Behind the
Berkshire Hathaway
Curtain

Behind the Berkshire Hathaway Curtain

Lessons from Warren Buffett's Top Business Leaders

Ronald W. Chan

WILEY
John Wiley & Sons, Inc.

Published by John Wiley & Sons, Inc., Hoboken, New Jersey.
Published simultaneously in Canada.

For general information on our other products and services or for technical support,
please contact our Customer Care Department within the United States at
(800) 762-2974, outside the United States at (317) 572-3993 or fax (317) 572-4002.

Wiley also publishes its books in a variety of electronic formats. Some content that appears
in print may not be available in electronic books. For more information about Wiley
products, visit our Web site at www.wiley.com.

ISBN: 978-0-470-56062-4

Printed in the United States of America

10 9 8 7 6 5 4 3 2 1

To my father, who always encouraged me to dream with my eyes open.

Contents

CONTENTS

Preface

"Success is not final, failure is not fatal: It is the courage to continue that counts"

—Sir Winston Churchill

Turning 30 years old at the time of writing this book, I reflect on my life so far and realize how fortunate I am. Having been raised in Hong Kong and having had the opportunity to study in America, I have managed to find a career that I truly enjoy, and I am grateful to have accomplished what I set out to achieve during my 20s.

While in college, I became interested in the stock market. My intention at first was to make some pocket money, but I was fascinated by the process of stock picking. My greatest satisfaction came from making the right investment decisions and carefully monitoring how my stock ideas played out.

After graduating with finance and accounting degrees from New York University in 2002, I had a few career opportunities but decided to follow my passion and learn more about investing. During the following year, I set up an investment partnership and made stock picking my full-time work.

Although conventional wisdom recommends that a fresh college graduate find a job and gain work experience, my decision to start a partnership was supported by my father wholeheartedly. He believed that my learning to become an investor could be a valuable experience, and getting a taste of it at a young age would be beneficial.

My father advised me that as long as I kept polishing my mind and acting sensibly I would do well eventually. He believed in my ability more than I believed in myself.

When I started my company, I had several partners who trusted me. I was not looking for superior investment performance at first. Rather, I wanted to prove my ability by aiming to build a sustainable operation. In that respect, I found Warren Buffett's value-investing philosophy most suitable for my style.

Value investing can be defined as finding an investment that sells at less than its intrinsic business worth. According to Buffett's mentor, Benjamin Graham, a value investment is "one which, upon thorough analysis, promises safety of principal and adequate return."

Buffett added to this definition when he said: "What is 'investing' if it is not the act of seeking value at least sufficient to justify the amount paid? Consciously paying more for a stock than its calculated value – in the hope that it can soon be sold for a still-higher price – should be labeled speculation."

The concept of value investing simply made sense to me, so I decided to pursue my business operation on the basis of those principles.

To strengthen my investment philosophy, I made my first trip to Omaha, Nebraska, to attend Berkshire Hathaway's annual meeting in 2003. My intention was to gain investment insights, but I found that Buffett, and his business partner, Charlie Munger, were discussing not only business and investing but also various other aspects of life.

A young man still searching for inspiration, I was highly influenced by their thinking. In my view, Buffett and Munger represented not only a value-oriented mind-set, but also a clear state of mind and personal well-being. As I learned more about their philosophy, I became a better investor by becoming a better person, and vice versa.

At that stage, as is still the case now, I had enjoyed every moment of my career. In Buffett's parlance, I tap-danced to work each morning.

Yet as I looked around and discussed my experience with my peers, I found that many of them were uncertain about their careers and what they wanted to pursue in life. Even if they had passion for something, there were always issues that held them back. Either they had mundane jobs but good salaries, or they were simply saving up their passion for a later time.

As the financial crisis hit the world in late 2007 and 2008, more of my peers became miserable about their professional and personal futures. I was just as uncertain, but I stayed positive and wanted to help make other people optimistic.

Then I had an idea: I wondered how successful people went through the early stages of their careers. If they could give business and life advice, what would they say? With that question in mind, I developed the concept for this book, from which I hope my peers and other professionals will be able to draw comparisons and use them as blueprints for their careers.

Exploring the concept further, I found Berkshire Hathaway the perfect organization for conducting such a project. It is a conglomerate with easy-to-explain operations that cover shoes, furniture, candies, building materials, energy, and even a newspaper.

Berkshire's executives are also passionate about their jobs. Coming from different walks of life and doing what they enjoy most in their industries, these business leaders promised to have many life lessons and business principles to share.

In late 2008, I wrote to Warren Buffett and explained my goals for the writing project. He quickly replied to me and said, "There is no reason not to pursue it!" With Buffett's positive feedback, I began to contact his executives individually. The task was daunting at first, but I was persistent, and they began to respond to my requests.

During the following year, I spoke to a total of nine executives and directors from Berkshire Hathaway. After visiting each of them, I noticed how they had different business and personal strengths from which we could learn.

For example, Randy Watson of Justin Brands discussed the importance of teamwork, and David Sokol of MidAmerican Energy Holdings touched upon the concept of discipline. I could not have learned more than I did from directly interacting with them.

Writing this book is a dream come true. I pursued the project because I believed that it was for a good cause. I told Buffett that I did not wish to profit from his fame, and part of the proceeds from the sale of the book will be donated to an education charity.

The main characters of this book are the leaders behind the curtain of Berkshire Hathaway. Through my journey of learning about their careers, I found out how they developed their skill sets in life and how their professional careers evolved over time. Their success has come in different forms.

Although this book may not offer investment advice like other Buffett-related books, it will offer you a sense of what life is, can be, or should be.

Ronald W. Chan
January 2010

Chapter 1

Exploring Life with Cathy Baron–Tamraz

Business Wire

"Life is either a daring adventure or nothing."
—Helen Keller

Business Wire is a leading global distributor of corporate news, regulatory filings, and multimedia. Via its patented online delivery platform, thousands of corporate press releases and filings are simultaneously transmitted to news media, financial markets, and information Web sites.

Its distribution network spans 150 countries and 45 languages, and partners with more than 60 international and national news agencies. Business Wire serves approximately 30,000 member companies and disseminates thousands of news releases.

Founded in 1961 by Lorry I. Lokey, a journalist and public relations executive, the company opened in San Francisco with seven presigned members and served local Bay Area media. Within four months, the company began to blossom and made its first profit.

In the 1960s, Business Wire formed affiliations with wires around the world and increased its member list. In 1967, it opened an office in Los Angeles, and by the end of the 1960s, the group had 15 employees and more than 300 member companies. The demand for financial information boomed in the 1970s, and the company opened offices in Seattle and Boston.

It is worth noting that in the late 1960s, 100 words per minute was the maximum speed for wire transmission, but in the 1970s, with satellite-to-computer delivery, news releases could reach end-users at 1,200 words per minute.

The 1980s were a decade of expansion for Business Wire. The company established a New York office, along with offices in 10 other locations. With 150 employees in 16 offices, the company's revenue base by 1990 was well past $10 million, placing it in the top tier of public relations service companies.

Business Wire entered the Internet age early with pioneering services and technology. It became the first commercial newswire to launch a website in 1995, and the up-to-date information it provided attracted more members. Its news content was featured on virtually every major search engine, web portal, and information service.

By 2000, the company had 26 offices, more than 400 employees and revenue approaching $100 million. In 2003, it even developed its own communication platform, dubbed "NX," to deliver encrypted corporate releases simultaneously to media and information systems around the globe. This innovation was awarded a U.S. patent in 2006.

When she became CEO of Business Wire in 2005, Cathy Baron-Tamraz, who joined the company in 1979, came upon an article about Warren Buffett in the *Wall Street Journal*.

The article, headlined "Buffett Unplugged" on November 12, 2005, described the type of companies for which the oracle of Omaha was looking. Inspired by what she read, Tamraz sent Buffett a letter explaining the company and asking whether or not he would be interested. To her surprise, Buffett called her one day and wanted to know more, so founder Lokey, CEO Tamraz, and Buffett met in San Francisco the following month.

Buffett liked the company and made an offer to Business Wire for an undisclosed amount on January 17, 2006. (It was believed that Business Wire had revenue of $127 million in 2005, and its appraised value at that time was about $600 million.) The deal was completed on March 1, 2006.

In Buffett's 2005 letter to shareholders, he wrote, "By the time I finished Cathy's two page letter, I felt that Business Wire and Berkshire were a fit. I particularly liked her penultimate paragraph: *'We run a tight ship and keep unnecessary spending under wraps. No secretaries or management layers here. Yet we'll invest big dollars to gain a technological advantage and move the business forward.'*"

Buffett further wrote that Business Wire, "like those of many entrepreneurs who have selected Berkshire as a home for their life's work, is an example of what can happen when a good idea, a talented individual and hard work converge."

As the company approaches its 50th anniversary, it continues to break new ground. Business Wire has been a pioneer in developing new XBRL financial reporting language and corresponding supporting services for corporations. It has also been a driving force in adapting to new channels of communications through its social media and search engine optimization platforms and products.

For this Berkshire star, the news is always breaking.

*C*athy Baron-Tamraz, the President and CEO of Business Wire, is one of the few female executives at Berkshire Hathaway. Many see Cathy as a hardworking and determined, yet friendly CEO, but during a meeting at her Manhattan office, she revealed her other qualities and the adventures she has had during her career.

⌘

Born in 1953 in Long Island, New York, Cathy had a suburban upbringing in a middle-class household. Her father, Murray Baron, was an engineer and her mother, Lillian, a housewife. Cathy believes she inherited her personality from her parents. She noted that her mother is soft spoken and easy going, and her father is tougher and more disciplined.

"I would say I have my affection for people from my mother and my street sense and principles from my dad," she said.

"Idle" was never a word Cathy's parents would use to describe her. Both athletic and an honor student at Mineola Public School in Long Island, she has always felt that life should be eventful and that staying within one's comfort zone discourages creativity.

With a natural sense of adventure and wanting to see what the world has to offer, Cathy packed her bags after graduating from high school and traveled across America. Upon her return, she attended the State University of New York.

When it came to choosing her college major, Cathy initially wanted to become a psychiatrist, but her parents were against it. They wanted her to study teaching because it is a respectable and stable profession. Cathy listened to their advice. As she also enjoyed reading and writing, Cathy opted for a double major in Education and English.

Cathy's curiosity and desire to explore the world never waned. She made the most of her summer vacations and traveled to different parts of Europe. Then one summer, she decided to try something different — cab driving.

She explained, "I came back from Europe in mid-summer, and I needed a job, so I became a taxi driver in the Long Island area. My parents weren't very supportive of the idea, but nevertheless it was an interesting experience for me. I even had the distinction of being the only female taxi driver at the time."

Cathy enjoys looking back at her various memorable experiences during college, some of which she has to laugh about. In fact, even Warren Buffett was impressed by her early adventures, noting that he was proud to have a Berkshire Hathaway executive who started out as a cab driver and eventually became the CEO of Business Wire. That is the American Dream.

Learning by Doing

Cathy realized that her liberal arts education gave her few business skills to apply at work in the beginning. However, she defended her college education and said, "I think a liberal arts education is invaluable in preparing one for the working world. I look at the people I have hired these past 30 years, and to be candid, most of them have had a more general background than a strictly business background."

She stressed that the college major one pursues is not the key; the whole idea of college is to learn about general principles by taking a variety of courses. Rather than screening for talent strictly on the basis of a person's college major, Cathy prefers to look for well-rounded, smart, and hardworking individuals who can make a solid contribution at work.

She said, "There is an old adage that goes 'you learn by doing!' I think that as you take on business projects and learn from your experiences, you learn new personal skills as your career unfolds." That said, Cathy believes that one must remain open to new ideas, stay flexible, and treasure teamwork in order to grow.

Cathy with Her Mother, Lillian Baron, in Hawaii
SOURCE: Used with the permission of Cathy Baron-Tamraz.

After college, Cathy worked as a high school teacher for some time but did not have a passion for the field, so she left and headed abroad again to search for her ideal career. On a stopover in Hawaii, she instantly fell in love with the island, so much so that she decided to stay there and find a job. She ended up in the tourism industry, becoming the manager of a boutique hotel.

Although she found it interesting to run a hotel business in an exotic location, Cathy ultimately felt that her career opportunities were limited and that she needed to move to a metropolitan area.

She explained, "I always wanted to travel after college, but I also knew I needed to focus on my career. After living in Hawaii, I decided to return home and continue my education. I ended up at Stony Brook University in New York, pursuing a master's degree in literature, with the thought of teaching at the college level."

After finishing graduate school, Cathy, along with her future husband, Stephen Tamraz, was asked to return to Hawaii and manage the hotel at which they had both previously worked. Shortly thereafter, the hotel was sold to a new owner, and in late 1979, the couple decided to move to a more traditional environment and settle down. They chose San Francisco — their favorite city — and sought new careers there. They married in 1982.

During her job search in San Francisco, Cathy saw a classified advertisement placed by Business Wire. Knowing that the job would involve editing, she answered the ad and joined the company in 1979. She became one of the editors of financial press releases that were distributed to the news media.

Then, in 1980, Cathy was asked to help open a new office in New York City. As her family lived in the area, and her future husband also had some entrepreneurial interests there, she decided to take up the opportunity and returned to New York. No one at the time would have guessed it, not even Cathy herself, but this was the real beginning of her career adventure.

Learning by Asking

Over the years, Cathy has also learned that the most direct way to learn is to ask. Although many people tend to be less vocal about their ideas, she has never been afraid to speak up and ask questions.

At Business Wire, Cathy not only wanted to do her own job well but also wanted to learn how the business worked. Company owner Lorry Lokey spent a lot of time explaining the industry to Cathy and, in many ways, became her mentor.

Discussing her relationship with Lokey, Cathy admitted that she was probably a pain for her boss at first. She confessed, "Lorry interviewed and hired me. As I was always curious about different decisions the company made or how the company worked, I asked a lot of questions. I was young and new to the business and somewhat 'feisty.' That might have annoyed Lorry at first, but it turned out to be very constructive!"

Cathy further added, "Lorry and I now laugh about how I gave him a bit of a hard time, but we both agree that sometimes you tangle with the person you end up having the greatest respect for. Because I was always interested in the business, Lorry must have admired my spunk, as he obviously targeted me for greater responsibility as my career developed."

Cathy learned from Lokey throughout her career, and she came to realize that it is crucial to build a business or a career one step at a time. Regardless of the pressure from naysayers or competitors, a person needs to be driven by long-term goals and to walk at her own pace. By remaining true to oneself and not being overly aggressive — and by this Cathy does not mean being conservative — one can set realistic goals that are far reaching, yet achievable.

She noted that Lokey taught her to remain competitive and to maintain an entrepreneurial spirit by taking calculated risks and trusting in her instincts. A good example is Lokey's decision to expand Business Wire in the 1980s. He was careful, yet fearless. He clearly outlined his goals and then pursued them without doubting his decision.

"Listening to your 'gut' is important! That does not mean stubbornness, but clearly and logically following your path. That ability requires courage," Cathy remarked.

> *Listening to your 'gut' is important! That does not mean stubbornness.*

Lokey, who is now in his 80s and retired, continues to impress Cathy by setting a good example. He is focused on giving away much of his earnings to charity to support education. Thus, he has shown Cathy that the circle of life is to learn, earn, and return.

Staying Open to Opportunity

Although Lokey gave her many growth opportunities, Cathy said that one important decision she made was also crucial to her future promotions at Business Wire: relocating to New York City. As the company was mainly a West Coast operation in the 1970s, to compete nationwide, Lokey decided to open an office in New York in 1980.

With a venturesome mind-set, Cathy took up the challenge to "go east." The courage to move changed her career prospects.

She elaborated, "I was about 26 at the time. I knew that if I performed well in the new location, I would be more easily recognized and rewarded than if I had stayed in our San Francisco location, which was then our headquarters. Although my career outlook was uncertain in New York, my instinct told me that I should just take the challenge and go for it. As a founding member of the New York office, I knew there would be a lot of opportunity in this critical market."

Cathy was initially a newsroom manager in New York. Within a few years, she had become head of the New York region. In 1987, she became eastern division manager, with overall responsibility for Business Wire's 14 eastern offices.

At 33 years old and climbing the corporate ladder as a female executive, overseeing the eastern division was a big challenge for Cathy. More people relied on her to make decisions, and because a number of older, male executives worked under her supervision, she knew she had to find a way to gain their respect and trust. She needed to show them that she was capable of doing the job and that she could be a strong and effective leader.

Drawing on her liberal arts background, Cathy realized that a book she had read earlier could help her to understand human relationships as she took on a leadership role.

She explained: "Joseph Campbell's *A Hero with a Thousand Faces* has had a profound influence on me. The book addresses the universal themes of different cultures, religions, and mythologies. Through it, I have learned that each of us is striving for the same things in the world. This understanding of the human condition has helped me to relate to my colleagues and clients."

In that sense, Cathy realized that understanding others is a key quality for a manager.

Cathy recalled that when she became the head of the eastern division, she called on each of the managers and told them about her new role and her new relationship with them. She explained that she would listen to their opinions and patiently make changes one at a time.

She said, "Although I had to prove to the team that I was capable, I also learned to be friendly while knowing when to keep a little distance to show my professionalism. I quickly analyzed the division and the personnel running each office, and I was then able to implement needed changes. Many of these managers still work for Business Wire today."

In 1990, Cathy was promoted to Vice President and also appointed to the company's Executive Committee. Following two more promotions in the following 10 years, she was eventually named Chief Operating Officer in 2000. In 2003, Cathy became President of the company and in 2005, Chief Executive Officer.

Having spent her entire career at Business Wire, Cathy said she never thought of trying out a different field, recognizing that there is no business like the news business. She is passionate about her job because the daily news flow is fast paced and the industry provides a service that requires constant upgrades and improvements to remain competitive. That level of excitement allows Cathy to stay engaged and to learn something new every day.

Do the Right Thing

Reflecting upon her career, Cathy said that of all the news that she has had to deal with over the years, the most difficult was the 9/11 terrorist attacks.

She described the incident: "Economically speaking, the financial crisis in 2008 is the worst I've seen, but emotionally speaking, 9/11 hit me a lot harder! I have dealt with all sorts of situations, but physically being in New York City when the planes hit the World Trade Center is something I'll never forget!"

Cathy paused for a moment, then she continued, "That day, I had two people working in the Wall Street area; after the attack, the first thought I had was 'Where are they?' We spent a good part of the day trying to locate them. Their cell phone reception was cut off, and this was a life and death situation! Luckily, our people were safe, but that day and the ensuing weeks were much more dramatic for me than the recent financial crisis."

Commenting on the fall of Wall Street and the Credit Crunch of 2008, Cathy said that business morals were completely disregarded, as money and greed blinded many people. As an example of how the world could be made a better place, she mentioned her favorite short story, O Henry's "The Gift of the Magi," which is about a husband and wife who give up their own treasure to buy each other a Christmas present.

"The story taught me about caring and how we should interact with one another," Cathy said. "Life is not just about receiving but also sacrificing and giving! Those who contributed to the recent crisis should read the story."

> *We are builders! We have the genes of going one step at a time.*

Cathy has never been tempted by quick profits or instant gratification, but embraced the corporate mentality of Business Wire: "We are builders! We have the genes of going one step at a time. Maybe we are naive, but we really don't know any other way of running a business than to do the right thing and make sure that we can all sleep at night."

She paraphrased Warren Buffett's quote, "Lose money for the firm, and I will be understanding. Lose a shred of reputation for the firm, and I will be ruthless."

Cathy Posing with Warren Buffett
SOURCE: Used with the permission of Business Wire.

The Art of Delegation

When Warren Buffett called Cathy to inquire more about Business Wire, she was shocked. "That moment is unforgettable!" she exclaimed, "Warren was so down to earth and unpretentious that the phone call wasn't even dialed in by his assistant. He asked me if I had a minute to chat, and then told me to address him as Warren. His casual attitude totally eased any anxiety."

Now that both Cathy and Business Wire have become part of Berkshire Hathaway, she feels that Buffett is inspiring not only as an investor but also as a person. "He's such a genuine and principled person. And his leadership skills are unsurpassed in that he inspires all of his managers to want to exceed his expectations. It truly is a privilege to be part of his team."

Although nothing has changed operationally since the acquisition, as part of Berkshire Hathaway, Business Wire has strong backing in terms of future acquisitions or aggressive business plans. That said, Cathy continues to run the company with the same disciplined approach she used prior to the acquisition.

Cathy Ringing the Opening Bell with Warren Buffett and the Business Wire Management Team
SOURCE: Used with the permission of NYSE Group Inc.

As the CEO, Cathy's main aim is to make sure that the company remains healthy and competitive. Her duty is to synchronize every division of the operation and set a clear business strategy for every employee to follow. After all, she is responsible for the careers of more than 500 people.

She is aware that both success and failure are essential ingredients for growth. No solid company can withstand the test of time without having gone through near-death experiences, Cathy believes. She has witnessed many ups and downs at Business Wire over the past three decades, and thus she remains careful but forward thinking, specially since the acquisition by Berkshire.

She said that true leaders who have been tested do not need to show off their abilities or create deals and "noise" for their company. They are the ones with discipline, solid business principles, and more important, a sense of team spirit that benefits the company as a whole rather than themselves as individuals.

> *True leaders who have been tested do not need to show off their abilities or create deals and "noise" for their company.*

Cathy admitted that she did not think about these business and personal qualities when she was young. She has realized that being at the top requires a strong temperament because vanity often blinds a person. She said, "An important ability is to learn how to delegate more. Letting go is sometimes hard, but it is necessary!"

Cathy also commented that advising employees and assigning jobs to them may sound easy, but spotting the right talent for the job and building a strong team to maximize a task are arts. She explained, "You have to let others learn by doing, and that is how you really see who can do the job."

Surprise Yourself!

One observation Cathy made is that talented people often underestimate their ability at first. The leader's job is thus to assign difficult, yet reachable, tasks to boost confidence while testing strengths and weaknesses.

"The cream naturally rises to the top," she said, "but while a leader needs to keep an open mind and patiently wait for young executives to grow, these people also need the determination to stick around with the company for the long haul. Otherwise, it doesn't matter how talented or intelligent the person is."

Noting that today's young generation has a marked tendency to switch jobs regularly, Cathy strongly advises young people to begin thinking about the long term and to persist in the same job, especially if they love the work and the company.

Remaining open minded and retaining the passion to explore means "you can be old at 40 but young at 80," Cathy said. "Having dealt with Lorry and Warren, and a few other wise men and women, I realized that their curiosity to learn keeps them young at heart."

"Obviously, hard work is always required to succeed, but being curious and adventurous enables you to challenge and surprise yourself," Cathy remarked. She has a favorite line that goes, "Do one thing each day that scares you!" By this, she does not mean to imply that one should be impetuous, but rather that testing limits and daring to be adventurous can certainly change a person's life.

Cathy concluded, "A lot of times after you have done something right, you think life is starting to get easy, but it doesn't work that way, so stay on guard with the spirit of an explorer!"

Chapter 2

Teaming Up with Randy Watson

Justin Brands

"There is no limit to what a man can do or how far he can go if he doesn't mind who gets the credit."

—Ronald Reagan

Widely known as the "Standard of the West," Justin Brands makes high-quality cowboy boots. The business was founded by Herman J. ("Joe") Justin, a leather craftsman from Indiana who moved to Spanish Fort, Texas, in the 1870s and began his tailored boot making and repair business in 1879.

Borrowing $35 from a local barber to start the company, Justin sold 120 pairs of custom-made boots at $8.50 apiece in the first year.

Justin's quality products and sharp business sense enabled the business to grow. After a few years, his seven children joined the boot-making operation, and his wife Annie contributed by developing a made-to-measure kit, thus enabling customers to order boots by mail.

With America's growing railroad network, Justin decided to expand the family business by moving closer to a railroad station, so in 1889 he relocated the operation to Nocona, Texas.

In 1908, Justin's sons John and Earl became partners, and the company changed its name to H. J. Justin and Sons. By 1910, their famous boots were selling at $11 a pair in 26 states and in other countries, including Mexico, Cuba, and Canada.

After Joe Justin passed away in 1924, his sons decided to make their second and final move to Fort Worth, Texas, to gain access to better railroad, postal and banking facilities, and a larger labor force.

A small conflict arose during the transition, when Joe's daughter Enid decided she did not want to relocate. She stayed behind and started up the Nocona Boot Company, which eventually became Justin's largest competitor.

Despite the Great Depression, which began in 1929, cowboy boots remained in style because of the popularity of western movies and culture, and Justin's business continued to expand. John Justin, the brother in charge, decided to increase the company's product offering to include field and laced boots.

This turned out to be a costly decision, and the company faced a number of difficult challenges in 1949. John's son, 32-year old John Justin Jr., believed that he could turn the business around, so he joined the family operation and took charge.

John Jr.'s first move was to acquire his uncle Avis's shareholding of the company, which turned him into the majority owner.

Knowing that cowboy boots had to keep up with trends, he designed and introduced a new model called the "roper," which featured a rounded toe that made it easier for rodeo performers and competitors to dismount their horses. The new boots were a big hit, starting the "urban cowboy" trend. Appointed company President in 1951, John Jr. improved the company's quality and service by enhancing its communication with retailers and using different marketing techniques to attract consumers.

In 1968, John Jr. sold the operation in exchange for stock in the First Worth Corporation, the parent company of Acme Brick. In 1972, this mini-conglomerate changed its name to Justin Industries. John Jr. was the leading figure in the new group, and under his leadership it bought his Aunt Enid's Nocona Boots in 1981, increasing its production to 8,000 pairs of boots a day.

In 1985, the group acquired the Chippewa Shoe Company of Wisconsin, allowing it to expand into sport and work boots. In that year, the footwear division's sales reached $103.9 million.

The group's success soon made it a takeover target. With the footwear unit generating $181.4 million in sales and the brick business, $118.9 million, corporate raiders targeted Justin Industries, the parent company of Justin Brands and Acme Brick, in 1990.

John Justin Jr., who was then in his 70s and owned 20 percent of Justin Industries, decided to defend his empire. He cannily purchased a troubled competitor, Tony Lama Company, with $18 million in cash and took on its $35 million debt load. The deal not only fended off corporate raiders but also strengthened the company's product line and growth prospects.

By 2000, Justin Boots had a 35 percent share of the $450 million U.S. market for western boots. That same year, Warren Buffett of Berkshire Hathaway purchased the group for roughly $600 million. John Justin Jr. was ill at the time, but he managed to oversee the transaction before he passed away a few months later.

Randy Watson, a 30-year veteran of the western industry (16 of them with Justin), remained in charge of Justin Brands after Berkshire Hathaway's acquisition in 2000.

Buffett likes to say that he can supply only cash but not management, so he told Watson to stay in Fort Worth and continue to do what he does best. Indeed, Watson has been autonomous ever since, and under his leadership, Justin Brands has become the number one choice in cowboy boots.

"*We are given two eyes, two ears, and one mouth, so we should always observe and listen, and talk only 20 percent of the time," said Randy Watson, President and CEO of Justin Brands. Although a cowboy may be viewed as a free spirit and individualistic character, Randy has learned to be a team player. Having been in the western industry for more than 30 years, he prefers to listen first and then ask questions.*

At the Justin Boots headquarters in Fort Worth, Texas, Randy discussed the essence of team spirit and his career ups and downs.

Born in 1957 in Austin, Texas, Randy joined Justin Brands as a sales manager in 1993 when he was 36 years old. "I took a fifty-six percent pay cut to take the job. Pretty smart, huh?" he joked in his Texan accent.

To defend his decision to take the cut, Randy used a sports analogy, "I would rather take less and play for the best team than get more and play for an average team."

He then explained, "Justin is a brand everyone in the western industry aspires to work for. Its culture and heritage date back to 1879, and its products are so premium that they are really the top brand for cowboy boots! Besides, John Justin Jr., the owner of the company, was a respectable man. Working for the man and the brand was something I had always wanted."

Randy believes that joining Justin was a logical decision, and it was indeed the best career move he ever made. He pointed out that when one is pursuing a career, it is important to consider not only the immediate prospects and trade-offs of the job but also its long-term potential and whether it fulfills one's ambitions.

He believes that finding the right company to work for and retire from is more crucial than receiving a higher salary.

For The Love of Baseball

In his youth, Randy kept his feet on the ground and did not blindly pursue his other dream: baseball. He gave up on the sport after college because he was not the kind of player he thought he should be.

When Randy talked baseball, his eyes lit up. He said, "My father played baseball at the University of Texas; then he played professionally in the Texas-New Mexico League. I basically grew up watching and playing baseball, so the sport is in my genes."

Randy said he enjoys the strategy and teamwork aspects of baseball, and therefore he wanted to coach or play professionally when he was young. "I basically majored in baseball in college! When I went to Wharton County Junior College in 1976, and then the University of Houston in 1978, I was switching majors between business administration and physical education," Randy confessed.

Randy Posing with Baseball Hall of Famer Nolan Ryan
SOURCE: Used with the permission of Justin Brands.

Randy initially wanted to be a coach, so he took physical education courses. Then, in the next semester, he felt he should be more realistic financially and began to study business administration. He knew that playing baseball was no longer feasible as a career, but then springtime came around, and he decided to take PE courses again to pursue a baseball coaching profession. This struggle lasted throughout college. Randy admitted that when he left school, his course credits were split between the two majors.

In the summer of 1980, when he was 23, Randy made his final attempt to pursue a career in baseball. He tried out at a few minor-league camps, but he did not make the cut on the first day of training. Returning to reality, he decided to look for a job and to compete in the business world rather than the sporting world.

Randy first worked as a part-time assistant at a western retail store called Don's Western Wear. It is worth mentioning that in 1980, the movie *Urban Cowboy*, starring John Travolta, was released hot on the heels of his hit *Grease*. With the movie grossing more than *Star Wars: The Empire Strikes Back* in the same year, it is little wonder Travolta started a craze for cowboy fashion.

Randy recalled, "Don's Western Wear was a few miles away from Gilley's bar, which was where *Urban Cowboy* was filmed. As cowboy fashion was the new trend, the store manager asked me to work as his assistant full time. I took his offer because I loved the product, and my aspirations for the game of baseball had come to an end. To be honest, it was just a job and I had no expectation to remain in retail whatsoever. However, my mind changed as my responsibilities grew."

Showing That You Care

At Don's, Randy started out as a salesman. He had to deal with customers and also he marketed the store's products. Within six months, he had become the store manager. His new post allowed him to travel and attend trade shows to meet with wholesalers, suppliers and manufacturers.

In 1982, Randy made a new commitment — he married Vicki Rush, whom he met through his colleagues at Don's. With a family to take care of, Randy wanted to explore new opportunities and seek career growth.

He decided to try out the wholesale side of the western business because he thought it had better prospects. He worked as a sales representative for various wholesalers over the next few years, including Nocona Boots (owned by Justin Brands) and Lucchese Boot, before finally landing his dream job at Justin Boots.

Reflecting on his early career, Randy has realized that he competed against himself to continue improving.

As a store manager, his goal was to buy the right products so the store would run better. Then, as a wholesale representative, he tried to excel by focusing on product design and marketing. Having experienced the western industry from such a wide angle, Randy's passion for it blossomed.

> *One thing I have learned is that people do not care what you know until they know that you care!*

"I came to like what I do because the people I deal with are really genuine folks. They are good people. Most of them value relationships, honesty, and integrity. Besides, a handshake with them still counts for something. All these years, I learned that when you work hard and are honest, people will embrace you," he said. "One thing I have learned is that people do not care what you know until they know that you care!"

Randy found that his sporting experience helped him in business, as he strove to remain competitive while contributing to the company. He also found the most joy and best experiences in cooperating and building a good team.

Randy explained, "In baseball or in business, it is never a one man show. Like baseball, before you surround yourself with the best players, you first have to compete to make the team, then you have to compete with your teammates so you can start on the team, then you have to learn how to work with your teammates to compete against other teams. I had that mentality with me all along, so I elevated myself by staying competitive, yet not alienating myself from others."

Joining Justin Boots, Randy felt that he had finally made it onto the best team in the league, and that he was a starter in the game. He started out as a batter, where he made it to first base as sales manager; then to second base as Vice President of marketing; and then to third base as division President of Justin Boots. Finally, in 1999, at the age of 41, he hit a home run and became President and CEO of Justin Brands, responsible for five different western brands.

The Benefit of Team Dynamics

Since becoming CEO, Randy's concern has been to make sure that everyone at the company pulls in the same direction and upholds the integrity and reputation of its brands. Just like in baseball, he cannot score a run if his teammates are not playing well, too.

After all, he remarked, brands take more than a century to build, but they can be destroyed in a moment.

Randy added, "I am very fortunate to lead a veteran team of professionals with longstanding and established brands. I learned that to run a company and be a leader, it is not about the individual, but how the team of people work together to accomplish something for the greater good. It is about working in unison. My job is to make sure that I have the right people in the right place, and then I stay out of their way."

> *My job is to make sure that I have the right people in the right place, and then I stay out of their way.*

Reemphasizing the fact that, to be a team leader and to build a good career, one must learn to listen and speak only 20 percent of the time, Randy noted that listening is an important interpersonal skill. It is not a passive process but active engagement. By listening, he has improved product quality and customer service, at the same time giving every employee a better place to work and from which to retire.

"If you listen," Randy said, "you give people strength and you instill confidence. When everyone can speak their mind, you give them the opportunity to contribute their best. Ultimately, everyone is happier and more positive, and you will be amazed what people will do for the company."

Randy acknowledged that good team work does not mean that everyone has to agree with one another. Indeed, he does not want people to agree with him just because of his position.

He believes that team members should agree or disagree during a discussion based on their beliefs. Surrounding oneself with good people means giving them the freedom to honestly and freely express their thoughts.

With that in mind, Randy welcomes healthy conflict and debate behind closed doors. He said, "Disagreeing is healthy, but that has to be done inside the room. When the team walks out from that room, everyone has to march out in unison and send a consistent message to the outside world. What is unhealthy is when team members walk out and undermine the decision of the group. I will not tolerate that."

The Courage to Lead

Speaking of decision making, one of the hardest calls that Randy and his team members have had to make was in 1999, when they had to close down two factories in one day. Justin Brands had decided to implement a new computer system to integrate all of its divisions and make the company more efficient and cost effective. Unfortunately, the execution of this system backfired.

As the company tried to track and synchronize everything from accounting and finance to inventory, purchasing, production, and personnel, instead of simplifying the entire operation, the new computer system complicated it.

Randy said, "We tried to implement the system such that we could monitor every boot style, size, and width, and even the colors of thread in every stitch pattern. If we were simply making white T-shirts, the system would have been great, but we were much more than that. Our company basically went down for a horrible 18 to 24 months. Because of that, our competitors gained market share, and we had to make the tough decision to close down two of our five production factories in order to survive."

From that experience, Randy learned that keeping a business simple is always the best policy.

Although the computer system now enhances Justin's productivity, getting through the implementation crisis was difficult for Randy. During this worst of times, one of his mentors, J. T. Dickenson, the ex-President and CEO of Justin Industries at the time it owned both Acme Brick and Justin Brands, spoke to him about what it takes to be a leader.

Dickenson handed him a speech given by President Theodore Roosevelt in 1910: "The Man in the Arena." One passage gave Randy the courage to do what was necessary, and it also taught him to step up and act like a true leader. It reads as follows:

> It is not the critic who counts: not the man who points out
> how the strong man stumbles or where the doer of deeds

could have done better. The credit belongs to the man who is actually in the arena, whose face is marred by dust and sweat and blood, who strives valiantly, who errs and comes up short again and again, because there is no effort without error or shortcoming, but who knows the great enthusiasms, the great devotions, who spends himself for a worthy cause; who, at the best, knows, in the end, the triumph of high achievement, and who, at the worst, if he fails, at least he fails while daring greatly, so that his place shall never be with those cold and timid souls who knew neither victory nor defeat.

Even after more than 10 years, the decision to close down those two factories still haunts Randy. He said he will never forget the scene when the factories were closed and about 500 workers were about to be let go.

Nevertheless, Randy faced up to reality and showed courage. He reminded himself that even if the decision was both gut wrenching and heartbreaking, the organization would be stronger as a result of it.

Coaches for Life

Having great respect for Dickenson and also for John Justin Jr., Randy often asks himself and his team a hypothetical question: "What would Justin Jr. or Dickenson do?" If they can answer the question comfortably, then chances are that they are making the right decision for the company.

In Randy's eyes, both men had an uncanny way of stimulating their employees. They asked easy questions that had no simple answers. For example, Justin Jr. would walk up to Randy and ask him such questions as "Are all of our customers happy?" or "Are all of the boots being made right?" or "Are all of the salesmen working as hard as they can?"

Although these were simple questions, a yes or no answer would never be 100 percent accurate; therefore,

Randy always had to think deeper and analyze an issue further before answering either of these great men.

Randy with John Justin Jr. (middle) and J. T. Dickenson (right)
SOURCE: Used with the permission of Justin Brands.

Another great man who has influenced Randy in the years since 2000 is Warren Buffett. Randy has a picture of Warren Buffett walking side by side with Arnold Schwarzenegger hanging on the wall of his office.

On the photograph, Buffett wrote "Gotta put Arnold in a pair of Justin's!" Thanks to the wit and support of the sage of Omaha, Randy is proud to be a part of the Berkshire family. He noted that any change in Justin's ownership after more than 100 years of operation would normally be cause for concern. Under Berkshire's ownership, however, there have been no problems.

Buffett leaves the management and day-to-day decision making to managers who are passionate about what they do, which is something that rarely happens in the corporate world.

Randy stated, "Unlike Berkshire, many corporate raiders never seem to leave good businesses alone. They feel the need to make changes even when a business has worked perfectly well for generations. It is funny how these raiders want to see results in a short period when they should notice that tested and true businesses take years to build!"

Randy realizes that Buffett knows how to keep complicated matters simple and that he understands that simple behavior is most effective in most aspects of life.

Although the world generally recognizes Buffet as a genius of the financial world, Randy also thinks that he is a brilliant marketer: he sells the incredible features and benefits of Berkshire ownership, and that attracts the willingness of like-minded business owners and other good companies to be part of the Berkshire family.

Returning to Frugality

Looking back, every step seemed easy and well calculated; but looking forward, everything appears to be very challenging.

As the team leader of Justin, Randy focuses on the long term. He admitted, "Looking back, every step seemed easy and well calculated; but looking forward, everything appears to be very

Randy Posing with Warren Buffett
Source: Used with the permission of Justin Brands.

challenging." The housing and economic crisis in 2008 have certainly hindered Randy and his team from looking too far ahead. However, they remain optimistic.

Randy argued that the western business has always been resilient in tough economic times. "Our products are not big-ticket items. In a downturn, people still spend on a few things that quench their buying desire. If a person thinks of getting a pair of cowboy boots, [he] (for parallelism in number) can still get them because they are affordable," he commented.

Reviewing the situation in the early 1980s, Randy stated that when *Urban Cowboy* set the trend, the business performed well despite inflationary fears and double-digit interest rates.

Randy with His Longhorn-Riding Crew Promoting Justin Brands
SOURCE: Used with the permission of Justin Brands.

Then, when America was hit with the Savings and Loan Crisis, which was followed by a recession from 1990 to late 1992, the overall industry continued to grow; 1993 was even a record year for Justin. Randy said, "The gratifying feeling of getting a pair of Justin Brands' boots makes a person walk talker and more proud, especially in difficult times!"

Speaking of the current crisis, Randy advises that money management is important. He believes that an economic crisis represents an opportunity for the world to return to frugality.

He constantly reminds his three children, Ryan, Reed, and Rachel, that they must learn to wait and save before they buy anything, even if it is a pair of Justin Boots. Randy said, "Staying out of debt is what the new generation must learn."

A Meaningful Life

A loving father and an active participant in community service, Randy puts a lot of his energy into children and education.

To name just two of the organizations with which he is involved, Randy is director of the Texas Ranger Association Foundation, which provides college scholarships for the children of Texas Rangers (not the baseball players but those who work in public safety), and is a director of the Texas FFA Foundation, which trains youths in critical thinking and communication skills, teamwork, and the development of a work ethic.

Also, as a past School Board President, Randy enjoys helping the younger generation. He has noticed that many people today work so hard that they disregard other aspects of life. Striking a balance between life and work is key to a meaningful life, he believes.

He said, "Working hard is good, but, please if you have children, remember to attend all your children's events! You can have 30 or even 50 years with a company, but your kids only go through first grade once. You have to understand that their childhood does not last very long, so if they engage in something, be there and enjoy the moment. Find places to work which give you that opportunity."

Randy promotes team spirit not only at work, but also in his personal life. In closing, this consummate Texan quoted a line from Henry Ford: "Coming together is a beginning. Keeping together is progress. Working together is success!"

Chapter 3

Taking Action with Stanford Lipsey

Buffalo News

"Never mistake motion for action."

—Ernest Hemingway

The *Buffalo News* is the dominant newspaper in Buffalo and its neighboring suburbs in New York State. Founded as the *Buffalo Sunday News* in 1873 by Edward H. Butler, it became the *Buffalo Evening News* in 1880.

From 1914, the *News* and the *Buffalo Courier*, its only competitor, operated under an understanding that the *News* would publish only Monday to Saturday evening editions. The *Courier* would publish morning editions, including one on Sunday.

Over the following few decades under the Butler family, the *News* became a force in Buffalo. It won several Pulitzer Prizes, including awards to Bruce Shanks for editorial cartooning for "The Thinker" in 1957 and to Edgar May for a series of articles on New York State's public welfare services in 1961. In 1989, Tom Toles won a Pulitzer for cartooning.

As Sunday circulation and advertising grew, the *News* found itself at a disadvantage with no Sunday paper. Thus, after Warren Buffett's Berkshire Hathaway purchased the paper for $32.5 million in 1977, he decided to publish a Sunday edition.

This new strategy was quickly opposed by its competitor. The *Courier-Express* filed a lawsuit against it for violating the Sherman Antitrust Act, citing seemingly unfair business practices such as offering subscribers the Sunday edition at a predatory rate, which in fact was incorrect.

After hearing Buffett's defense of the *News* in court and his rationale for the changes, the judge allowed the paper to continue publishing its Sunday edition but imposed an injunction that limited its ability to market and promote itself.

The ensuing newspaper war became so intense that the viability of the *News* was at stake and Buffett asked Stanford Lipsey, an old friend and a veteran of the Omaha newspaper industry, to travel to Buffalo to oversee the business as a consultant.

In 1979, the U.S. Court of Appeals reversed the earlier injunction on the *News*, stating that "all that the record supports is a finding that Mr. Buffett intended to do as well as he could with the *News* and was not lying awake thinking what the effect of its competition on the *Courier* would be. This is what the antitrust laws aim to promote, not to discourage."

In 1982, the paper's only rival, the *Courier-Express*, ceased publication. The *Buffalo Evening News* then shortened its name to the *Buffalo News* and began publishing both morning and evening editions until 2006, when the evening edition ceased publication. All along, Stanford Lipsey has been the key man at the *News*. He was named Publisher and President of the paper in 1983.

With a long-standing commitment to quality news reporting, the *Buffalo News* states its goal clearly: "We want to be a paper that consistently executes important investigations and journalism, presented effectively and with style; that engages readers and makes itself indispensable to them; and that is shot through with intelligence, sophistication, and humanity."

*S*tanford Lipsey summed up his passion for the newspaper industry by quoting a line from Thomas Jefferson: "When the press is free and every man able to read, all is safe."

The Publisher of the Buffalo News *and a longtime friend of Warren Buffett and Charlie Munger, Stan is the most experienced and longest-serving executive of Berkshire Hathaway. Now in his 80s, but still with a sharp nose for news, Stan divides his time between Buffalo in New York and Palm Springs in California.*

Stan visits California a few times a year to avoid the long, cold Buffalo winters. He has an office set up in his getaway home, from which he coordinates closely with his East Coast colleagues while away. In his Palm Springs office, Stan sat down to share his life story, his tremendous experience of the newspaper business, and comment on his friendship with Warren Buffett.

Born in Omaha, Nebraska, in 1927, the "newsman," as Stan often calls himself, lived through the best and the worst of America's twentieth century. Growing up during the Great Depression in the 1930s and living through World War II, Stan never felt deprived of anything.

He said, "In the old days, there was a saying that 'Uncle Sam will take care of you!' When I grew up, our world was smaller and people were not as sophisticated. During the 1930s, sources for news were not as abundant as today. We did not know as much about the outside world and life was very simple."

Stan had a normal childhood. Given a camera to play with when he was 10, he immediately fell in love with photography, a passion that would be his for life. During his years at Central High School in Omaha, he was the photographer for the school newspaper and later a photographer and photography editor at the University of Michigan.

He commented, "Somehow I find photography so rewarding that I can entirely focus myself on it and forget other concerns. It's not just a hobby but a way to artistically express myself and relieve pressure."

Aside from his interest in photography, Stan admitted that he had little idea of what he wanted to do in life while at college. Having no direction in which to head, he decided to study economics so that he could gain a general sense of business. Eager to enter the real world to search for his life's passion, Stan graduated from the University of Michigan in only three years.

At the age of 20 in 1948, he knew more about what he did not want to do than what he did. His father owned a wholesale meat and poultry firm and was planning to retire. He asked Stan if he wanted the business, but Stan decided that would not be his life's work, so his father sold the business and Stan moved to Los Angeles.

While searching for a job in Los Angeles, Stan kept in mind that whatever field he went into, he would need to learn how to sell. He explained that all businesses operate by selling something, whether it is tangible or intangible. Therefore, to succeed in any field, sales and marketing ability is essential.

Stan accepted a sales job at Libby, McNeill & Libby, marketing its baby-food line and selling it to grocery stores while he and his father looked for a business they could buy and operate. However, after two years in the position, Stan felt that was not going to happen in Los Angeles.

He explained, "I was turning 22 years old at the time. I felt that a big city like Los Angeles was too competitive for a fresh college graduate to find a business to buy. I knew about an opportunity selling advertising for a weekly newspaper called the *Sun* in Omaha, so I returned to my hometown."

Finding a Focus

The newspaper business offered many facets of interest and influence for Stan. His new responsibilities enabled him to deal with many types of clients, and the industry provided him with the opportunity to learn about other types of businesses. As it turned out, the newspaper industry was the most fascinating for Stan, so he decided to stay on.

However, just as he was beginning to appreciate his new job, the Korean War broke out in 1950. Stan was soon called up to serve in the U.S. Air Force and was assigned to be newspaper editor at the Strategic Air Command Headquarters at Offutt Air Force Base near Omaha. Shortly afterward, he was ordered to go to Korea, but an unusual incident held him back.

Stan told the story this way: "One day an officer from the Office of Strategic Investigations, which was like the FBI of the air force, took me to its headquarters and grilled me on a case involving another airman named Jim Clements, who had shared an air force plane ride with me to New York and then to a school on David's Island off the coast of New Rochelle. While we were supposed to turn in our per diem tickets before the plane ride, which I did, Clements sold his to someone else and forged his way on to the air force plane taking us to New York. He got caught. Since I was the main witness in the case, I was taken off orders to go to Korea so I could be at the trial."

The trial worried Stan. During questioning, the officer threatened him, noting that he would be sent to prison at Fort Leavenworth to "turn big rocks into small ones" if he did not cooperate with the investigators. He made it through the court-martial, and Clements was acquitted on a technicality.

Soon thereafter, Stan was released from the air force on a hardship discharge because his father had become seriously ill. When Stan was still only 24, his father passed away.

Arriving back in Omaha, Stan rejoined the *Sun*. Having made up his mind that the newspaper business was the career for him, he rotated among various departments, working first as photographer, then reporter, then editor. He learned about advertising, production, and circulation while expanding the paper.

In the 1950s, the company that owned the *Sun* had two newspapers covering two parts of town. Now an executive, Stan recognized that if the company bought the papers covering other parts of town, he would have the opportunity to sell advertising citywide. So he bought them, allowing the *Sun* to expand its clientele and increase both volume and profit.

Stan believes that selling involves understanding what the customer needs and the art of persuasion. Taking the client's perspective allows the salesperson to think strategically and speak logically. "A salesman must believe in his product; otherwise how can he speak with conviction?" Stan asked.

He also believes that patience and persistence are required, because those who are not convinced at first may yet become interested in the future: "As an advertising executive, I learned to be observant and flexible. I learned to pick up information from my clients so that I could prepare data to attract them. As the saying goes, 'persistence succeeds when all else fails!' I just kept trying and trying."

> *As the saying goes, 'persistence succeeds when all else fails!' I just kept trying and trying.*

Stan's career at the *Sun* blossomed. Selling advertising; understanding employees, clients, and politicians; trying different strategies; brainstorming news ideas; and expanding the business all represented career growth. In the mid-1960s, he became Publisher and majority owner of the newspaper.

Buffett for Life

Reflecting on his success at the *Sun*, Stan said that it was really about trial and error. Without a mentor to look up to, he gained experience the hard way. In this respect, he advises the younger generation to find mentors from whom they can benefit.

For Stan, a mentor is someone who can enhance a person's growth and help him or her avoid making mistakes or wasting time, whether in life or at work.

"Fortunately," he remarked, "I found a mentor later in my life, who became a role model and a resource for me to learn from and share with: Warren Buffett."

Stan met Buffett's late wife Susan before he met Buffett. Both were jazz lovers who had helped to form an Omaha group that lobbied various organizations to sponsor jazz in the community. In 1965, when Stan was Publisher and President of the *Sun*, Buffett approached him and asked whether the company was for sale.

Stan at first declined the offer because he had no idea who Buffett was. After getting to know the man, he began to admire Buffett's knowledge of the newspaper business. In 1969, just after Stan had turned 42, he decided to sell the *Sun* to Buffett.

Stan not only received cash from the sale but also gained the opportunity to become one of the last participants in Buffett's investment partnership. The long-term relationship between Stan and Buffett began in this period, and they have been business associates, partners, and friends ever since.

Buffett made no changes to the *Sun*'s management team, and Stan continued to run it. However, he and Buffett often discussed ideas and searched for ways to increase the paper's circulation. In the early 1970s, they decided to emphasize investigative journalism.

Stan recalled, "Our papers were area specific. Some of the news was common to all, so Warren and I came up with the idea to add fresh news to our publication by initiating

Stan (right) and Warren Buffett on the Purchase of the *Sun* in 1969
SOURCE: Used with the permission of Stanford Lipsey.

investigative reporting. This would be our niche because no other publications were pursuing it. We became a force in the community, and it was rewarding that people were interested in what we wrote."

In 1972, the idea paid off, and the pair received public recognition for it. Stan, Buffett, and Editor Paul Williams shared a Pulitzer Prize for local investigative reporting. They uncovered the large financial resources of Boys Town in suburban Omaha, which later led to reforms of its charitable organization.

Buffett had more in store for "the newsman." In 1977, when Berkshire Hathaway acquired the *Buffalo News* in upstate New York, Buffett knew that the business required an extreme makeover, and he asked Stan to help.

Stan was initially uncomfortable with the idea of moving to Buffalo, but Buffett asked him if he could simply visit the place one week every month to overlook the business, and Stan accepted that option.

The Satisfaction of Accomplishment

Stan commuted to Buffalo as a consultant to improve the newspaper's circulation and strengthen its advertising department. The new opportunity gave Stan a sense of accomplishment, and he began to enjoy his involvement with the *News*.

> *I thrive on the satisfaction of accomplishment . . . the feeling of getting things done gives me passion in life and in business.*

He remarked, "I thrive on the satisfaction of accomplishment. It can be closing a sale, or it can even be cleaning the closet at home, but the feeling of getting things done gives me passion in life and in business. Warren once said to me that I am a doer. I never thought about that, but then I really like initiating projects and getting them done."

During his monthly visits, the challenges at the *News* excited Stan. There were many problems, but Stan built a strong management team and initiated a number of new sources of revenue.

He remained careful and logical but also came up with inventive angles to improve sales and circulation. He knew that being the market place for advertising was the key to the paper's survival, and thus he applied the strategies that he and Buffett developed at the *Sun* to accomplish that.

One major achievement was the creation of the *Home Finder*, a tabloid-style real estate guide. This guide not only became a hit in the community and a major revenue source for the paper but also moved all the real estate advertising from the competition to the *News*.

By 1980, Stan had come to enjoy working in Buffalo, and he decided to make a permanent move to the city. On June 6, he left the *Sun* in Omaha and officially became Vice Chairman and Chief Operating Officer of the *Buffalo News*. Two years later, he assumed the role of Publisher and President.

After working full-time to improve the quality of the *News*, Stan wanted to stay informed on all fronts. He involved more middle-management executives in the decision-making process and encouraged everyone to speak up. He also organized company activities to allow employees to network and share opinions. At one company picnic, Warren Buffett made a surprise visit and mingled with everyone.

Stan changed the culture of the *Buffalo News*. Its employees became more vocal, energetic, and passionate about their jobs, and the paper gained a positive image among both employees and locals as not just a news provider but also a force in the community.

In 1989, Buffett wrote in his annual letter to shareholders that "Stan's managerial skills deliver at least five extra percentage points in profit margin compared to the earnings that would be achieved by an average manager given the same circumstances." That amounts to several million dollars a year and sums up Stan's ability.

For his part, after having known Buffett for more than 40 years, Stan believes that the man not only is brilliant but also has an incredible memory, good judgment, and is totally ethical. He said, "Warren's ideas are always sound, and he is able to take complicated situations and reduce them to a very simple understanding."

Indeed, Stan said that one reason he is still working is because he wants to continue his association with Buffett. "It's interesting that people who sell their businesses to Berkshire and no longer own them work even harder because they admire Warren so much that they just want to become better managers."

The Newsman in Action

Stan believes that newspapers are one of society's most important institutions. He realizes that the Internet and other media channels threaten the industry, but he is hopeful because most of the news is created by newspaper reporters.

"The niche now," Stan said, "is for regional newspapers to deliver quality local news. This is the competitive edge local newspapers, such as the *Buffalo News,* have. National papers simply do not have that capability."

He explained, "A newspaper must reflect its constituency by providing relevant, accurate, and fair reporting to readers. We also need to provide investigative reporting to improve our society as a whole. If we don't do it on behalf of our readers, who will?"

Stan has certainly helped improve his surroundings outside of his role at the *News.* For example, he has organized an annual free jazz series at the Albright-Knox Art Gallery since 1981. It's the longest-running series of its kind in the country.

Speaking of his love of jazz, he said, "I think every generation grows up with their own idiom. Jazz is America's only original art form. I am not a good musician, but having a personal link to it by organizing these concerts to promote jazz has added a great deal of pleasure to my life."

In 1989, he received the New York State Governor's Arts Award for his ongoing support of New York cultural institutions.

Stan also serves the Buffalo community by helping to restore some of its best-known landmarks. For example, he has dedicated thousands of hours and raised $14 million for the restoration of the Darwin Martin House Complex in Buffalo, which was designed by architect Frank Lloyd Wright. It is the largest and most costly renovation of a Frank Lloyd Wright property in the world.

In the 1990s, Stan teamed up with the Governor of New York, the state's two senators, and many others to raise the millions needed to acquire the property and restore it to its original 1907 condition. In 1998, he received the Governor's Award for Historic Preservation.

In 2001, at the age of 74, Stan voluntarily gave up his role as President of the *News* but still retains the title of Publisher. In 2005, the University of Michigan honored him for his contribution to the newspaper industry, naming its student publication building after him, a fitting reward for this consummate newsman.

Reviewing his career, Stan said he believes that his achievements have far exceeded the dreams of his youth. After graduating from college, he expected merely to find a decent job and to live a rather mundane life. By working at the *Sun* and then the *Buffalo News*, however, he had the opportunity to initiate important stories and to influence public life.

Stan noted that finding the right career early in life is often difficult. He feels that if he had been able to take part in internships during college, he would have felt less uncertain about his career and been able to identify the right field at an earlier age.

Stan Sharing an Ice-Cream Moment with the Author
SOURCE: Used with the permission of Ronald Chan.

> *I recommend the younger generation look for internships and get a taste of the real world.*

"Speaking from experience, I recommend the younger generation look for internships and get a taste of the real world. It's important to put real life opportunity in perspective and crystallize where one's interests lies," Stan commented.

To support the younger generation, he actively welcomes and supports interns at the *Buffalo News*. He said, "If you are a college intern at the *News* and you write a good story, your name appears in the paper. An achievement like that is often an encouragement, and it helps one grow as a person. Plus, it gives you a clearer mind-set of whether you want to go into newspapers."

Talking about what else he might have done in life, Stan joked that he wishes he were a better golfer or tennis player, because many of his friends, including Buffett, are far better athletes than he is. However, his artistic side, especially his talent as a photographer, means more to him than sports.

One of Stan's Favorite Photographs Taken at the Main Street Post Office in Buffalo, New York
SOURCE: Used with the permission of Stanford Lipsey.

Stan has held 10 photographic exhibitions. One particularly rewarding show involved 43 of his photographs (some of which were 11 to 12 feet long) in the radiation wing of the Roswell Park Cancer Institute in Buffalo. The patients told him that they appreciated his work tremendously and that it had a very positive affect on them.

A few years later, a friend recommended that Stan publish a book of his photography. The *Affinity of Form*, published in June 2009, compares pairs of his photographs. Stan said he wanted to explore how his various pictures

Stan's Fascination with Geometric Shapes Emerges Again in This
Photograph of the Rookery Building in Chicago, Illinois
SOURCE: Used with the permission of Stanford Lipsey.

were similar to or different from one another in terms of
form, texture, and color composition.

Hanging in his Palm Springs residence are four photographs of an oak tree in Delaware Park that Stan took
during the four seasons. Although it may appear that these
photos were easy to take, he spent many years patiently
taking numerous shots to get the ones he wanted. He said,
"The accomplishment is not only the end result; it's also
the process of actions leading to the right conclusion. The
same is true for life!"

Chapter 4

Brainstorming with Barry Tatelman

Jordan's Furniture

"The world is but a canvas to the imagination."
—Henry David Thoreau

The founder of Jordan's Furniture, Samuel Tatelman, was a Russian immigrant and shoemaker who settled in Manchester, New Hampshire. He began operating a furniture business from the back of a truck in 1918. A few years later, he officially opened his first store with his brother-in-law in Waltham, Massachusetts.

In 1928, Samuel decided he wanted to run his own business, and so he formed Jordan's Furniture. Although no one knows exactly how he chose the name, Samuel is thought to have shuffled several names in a hat and randomly pulled out "Jordan's."

Samuel's son, Edward, joined the business in the 1930s. Surviving the Great Depression and then the Second World War, Jordan's continued to do steady business, although it remained a small, local operation in the Waltham community.

The third Tatelman generation took over in the early 1970s. Eliot and his younger brother, Barry, became co-CEOs of Jordan's Furniture in 1973. They knew that if they wanted to promote Jordan's and grow the business, they would have to come up with new ideas to attract customers.

After a number of brainstorming sessions, they decided to advertise on the radio instead of in the local newspaper. Their rationale was to try something different, hoping to reach a wider audience. To save trouble, they even decided to record their own commercials. The strategy was an instant success, and the two brothers became local celebrities. Jordan's Furniture began to thrive.

In 1983, the duo opened a second Jordan's store in Nashua, New Hampshire. Then, in 1987, they opened a third, in Avon, Massachusetts.

Fun-loving, unconventional, and often creative, the Tatelmans firmly believed that the concept of "shoppertainment" was essential to attracting visitors. Without entertainment, they felt, furniture stores could be dull. Thus, they came up with innovative ways of attracting new visitors, especially families with children.

For instance, at one point, they wanted to install a Ferris wheel in one of their stores, but instead settled on a Motion Master, a rollercoaster-like, cinematic thrill ride. On Mother's Day in 1992, the brothers presented this new experience in the Avon store and called it a Motion Odyssey Movie.

In 1998, the Tatelmans opened a new location in Natick, Massachusetts. This time they wanted the shopping experience to be more like visiting a theme park, so they created a 120,000-square-foot showroom with a Bourbon Street theme.

While the Tatelmans were having fun and attracting numerous shoppers, their fame also caught the attention of competitors. The legendary Warren Buffett, who already owned three furniture companies at the time, asked his operating managers who they admired most in their industry. They all said "Jordan's."

That response led to a meeting between Buffett and the Tatelman brothers in August 1999. After realizing that Buffett was honest and had no intention of changing the company's structure, the brothers decided to sell their business to him.

They came to an agreement in mid-October of the same year. The exact terms of the sale have never been disclosed, but it is believed that the Tatelmans received between $225 and $250 million in cash.

Under Eliot and Barry's watch, Jordan's grew from 5 employees in 1 store to more than 1,000 in 4 locations in New England over just 25 years. On an average weekend, the Avon and Natick stores now attract more than 4,000 people.

Knowing that making money means corporate responsibility, Jordan's supports various charities to help the communities in which it operates. To name just two, the company provides strong support to Project Bread, which helps hungry people throughout Massachusetts, and works closely with the Massachusetts Adoption Resource Exchange, which helps foster children to find permanent homes.

In October 2006, Barry decided to retire after serving as co-CEO and co-President with his brother Eliot for 34 years. Although Eliot now runs the show, Barry occasionally chips in with ideas.

Jordan's marketing continues to impress. In March 2008, for example, Eliot promised customers who made a purchase between March 25 and April 27 that if the Boston Red Sox swept the World Series, they would receive their furniture for free. The promotion not only excited every Bostonian but also gave them all a reason to shop.

> Creativity clearly distinguishes Jordan's Furniture from its peers. With Eliot in charge and frequent creative contributions from Barry, more unexpected promotions are still to come!

*B*arry Tatelman is the co-owner and ex-CEO of Jordan's Furniture. Dressed in a relaxed polo shirt, blue jeans, and a pair of Converse sneakers as he entered the bar at the Taj Hotel in Boston, Barry looked like a creative director. At a table overlooking the Boston Common gardens — the country's oldest public park — the 34-year veteran of furniture retailing shared his unique marketing insights and true Bostonian story.

The youngest of three brothers, Barry was born in 1950 and grew up in Newton, Massachusetts. When he was a child, Barry's father, Edward, would come home at night and tell his sons stories about their family-owned furniture store — Jordan's Furniture in Waltham, Massachusetts.

Wanting to experience the family business firsthand, the sons worked at the store as part-time helpers during elementary school.

Eliot, the second brother, would receive 10 cents an hour to dust, and Barry, four years younger, received 5 cents an hour. Whereas Barry was always fascinated with the promotional side of the business, his brother Eliot enjoyed looking after the managerial side.

After attending Newton High School in his hometown, Barry decided to explore his artistic side by studying drama at Ithaca College in New York State. His initial dream was a professional acting career, but after completing his freshman year, Barry realized that drama was not for him after all, so he transferred to Boston University and majored in advertising and public relations. This decision was encouraged and inspired by his oldest brother, Milton.

Barry recalled, "Milton, who passed away in 1993, was always a mentor to me when it came to creativity. He used to produce advertising for motion pictures and different consumer products in New York City. After listening to Milton's stories and having him share his experiences with me, the subject interested me, so I decided to pursue advertising as my major."

Admitting that college was not very significant for him, Barry believes that his two internships were both more fun and educational. One year, he worked at a TV station, brainstorming ideas for commercials to be aired during local shows and news. The next year, he worked as a movie and theater critic for a local magazine called *People* (not the well-known *People* magazine). This internship experience was particularly meaningful for Barry, as he would later go into the theater business after retiring from Jordan's.

Although he may have found his activities outside college a better source of ideas and inspiration, his studies did give Barry the opportunity to meet his future wife, Susan Lobovits, in 1969. Sharing similar family values and life aspirations, the two decided to marry in 1973 when Barry turned 23.

After graduation, Barry was supposed to work at an advertising agency as a copywriter, but when he sat down with his father to discuss his career plans, he was asked to join his brother Eliot at Jordan's Furniture and to promote the store, which he did.

Barry recalled, "My father, Edward, taught us to learn from our mistakes. He gave us the responsibility many parents wouldn't. His concern was not whether or not we did things right or wrong but about giving us the confidence to run the business."

Barry confessed that even after having been a father himself for more than 30 years, he still sometimes finds it hard to let go of his kids and allow them to go their own way. He appreciates what his father did for him: "Because my father really stepped back, he allowed us to try things differently, and that is why Eliot and I became creative in our own sense."

Thinking Differently

In 1973, when Eliot and Barry officially took over the company, Jordan's Furniture was a small store with only a handful of employees. The two knew that if they wanted to start their own families and succeed in business, they would have to think big and promote the store regionally.

As most competing furniture stores were very similar at the time, they knew they needed to be distinctive to attract customers.

After mulling over different ideas to promote Jordan's, they decided to advertise using radio spots rather than print ads in local newspapers. Instead of ordinary radio advertisements, however, the two brothers came up with humorous scripts that caught listeners' attention.

They started out yelling and screaming over the radio to sell waterbeds, which was rather unconventional at the time, as were waterbeds themselves. Even their grandfather Samuel was surprised, phoning from Florida to ask if they were really selling "plastic bags full of water." Indeed they were — 25 water beds a day at $600 each.

Their promotional strategy was a big success, and Eliot and Barry soon became icons in their neighborhood.

Reflecting on working as a team with Eliot, Barry said, "My father taught us a good family principle: he said that family is always first, and no decision should cause the family to fight. With that motto, Eliot and I gelled really well. We learned that if we could put our strengths together, we could enhance the business while respecting one another."

Barry commented, "There were of course times when Eliot and I had different opinions, but knowing that every idea or inspiration could turn into an opportunity, I was not too concerned with whose idea was used. He could try his first, and then I could always try mine next. The fact is, no business issue is worth fighting over. Family should always come first!"

As Barry reflected on his working years with his brother Eliot, he noted that a movie called *Avalon* echoed their relationship. The movie follows a family of Eastern European immigrants pursuing the American Dream. Much the way that an emphasis on family values and preserving family memories runs through the heart of this movie, Barry feels that his greatest joy stems not from the success of their business but from the way they have always stood by each other over the years.

Barry explained, "There is a scene in the movie when the brothers open a department store. On the opening day they drive to the store and see a long line of customers waiting to get in. The brothers look at each other in awe and feel a sense of achievement. That scene is my favorite because it captures how Eliot and I felt as brothers and as business partners."

A Passion for Creativity

Prior to retirement, Barry acted as co-CEO of Jordan's, mainly responsible for advertising and promotions. Eliot handled merchandising, company systems, and related operational matters.

When it came to idea generation, the two would sit down and brainstorm. Their eldest brother, Milton, who created commercials for major films such as *The Godfather* and *Rocky*, would occasionally chip in ideas, too.

Eliot and Barry never wanted traditional radio or television commercials, and neither did they want to run a pure furniture business. They wanted to have fun in the process and to try something different each time. In a way, they wanted to surprise themselves.

Barry said, "We wanted our place to be a little out of the boundary, or out of the paradigm, and the image we built reflected on that."

Indeed, thinking outside the box not only allowed Jordan's to stand out but also gave Barry passion for his work. In his view, passion is the result when a person has the opportunity to do what he enjoys and does not get bogged down by red tape or meaningless corporate rules.

"The problem is," Barry explained, "many corporations have regulations and hierarchy that make people counterproductive. They knock down everyone's creativity, excitement, and thrills from what they enjoy doing."

"If an idea didn't sound too crazy to Eliot and me, we tried it. That gave us the passion to explore and to have fun. After all, we were selling furniture, and it wasn't a sexy business to begin with," Barry added.

Creativity, for Barry, is an important ingredient of Jordan's success. Although he believes that some people are born to be creative, it is also a skill that can be cultivated.

"I think everyone has a great amount of creativity. As long as they don't get pushed away by corporate rules, they can flourish. For example, one day our employees decided to dress up in tuxedos to impress customers, and the next day they decided to offer customers roses when they picked up their furniture. All these creativities add up to our image. While our employees enjoyed their work, customers also treated us with more respect," Barry explained.

I think everyone has a great amount of creativity. As long as they don't get pushed away by corporate rules, they can flourish.

On one occasion, Barry and Eliot decided to show gratitude to their 1200 employees. They wanted to boost everyone's morale, but they also wanted to add suspense to what they would do, so notices and clues were sent out to employees about a special date: May 10, 1999.

On that day the secret was revealed. The brothers closed the store, and the whole crew went to Bermuda for the day on a private plane. A commercial was filmed there while everyone was enjoying themselves and making sofas out of sand. The event not only drew massive media attention but also turned some of Jordan's employees into local celebrities.

Barry commented, "An event like that added passion to work and life. We indirectly promoted the store but also thanked our employees for their hard work."

Honesty and Sincerity Sell

Reviewing his career at Jordan's, Barry noted that success and crisis sometimes go hand in hand. When he turned 37 in 1987, Jordan's opened its third location in Avon, Massachusetts. Opening day caused the largest traffic jam ever seen in the town.

Barry said, "Our promotion went too well, and that, in itself, became a crisis. Everybody came to our store, and there was a two and a half hour wait in line. It was a cold February day, and as the customer flow got out of control, we went on the radio to beg people not to come. We even promised to keep our discount prices for weeks. It was a bad day, but we ended up turning it into another store promotion."

Truthful advertisements sometimes outsell those that are manipulative or inaccurate.

Barry admitted that being honest sometimes has an opposite effect than that intended. When he and his brother asked people not to go to their new store, more people showed up. In this respect, Barry believes that truthful advertisements sometimes outsell those that are manipulative or inaccurate.

In this vein, a movie that Barry said he especially enjoys is *Crazy People*, starring Dudley Moore as an advertising executive admitted to a psychiatric hospital after a mental breakdown. At the hospital, he is inspired by fellow patients to produce truthful advertisements, which are more successful than traditional advertising by being far more candid.

Honesty and sincerity win people's trust. When Warren Buffett became interested in learning more about Jordan's Furniture, his relaxed and honest nature struck a chord with the Tatelmans. When Buffett met the brothers in 1999, both parties were initially interested only in friendship.

Barry said, "Our mutual friend asked us if we could show Warren our stores while he was in Boston, so we picked him up at the Prudential Center. We went to the

Barry on Boston Common.
SOURCE: Used with the permission of Ronald Chan.

garage and could not find our car, so all of a sudden we were walking with the richest man in the world and searching for our car. The scene certainly made an impression."

After the meeting, Buffett told Eliot and Barry that if they were ever ready to sell their business, he would be interested in buying it. Buffett's comment led the Tatelmans to think about the future of Jordan's Furniture.

Barry elaborated, "We came to think about the next generation and how to be fair to the family. In fact, in any family business, being fair to everyone is important because money can really break up a lot of good family ties."

The brothers concluded that if they sold their furniture business to Buffett, the changes to the operation would be minimal, and at the same time it would be fair to all family members.

Their decision was the right one. Nothing changed after the deal went through, and the duo continued to do what they enjoyed doing. The only addition to the business was Buffett as a cheerleader, providing unconditional support and advice whenever they needed it.

To celebrate the sale of Jordan's, the brothers decided to give every staff member a bonus out of their own pockets: 50 cents for every hour they had worked for the company. This generous gesture cost them approximately $10 million, with one employee who had worked for the company for more than 18 years receiving more than $40,000.

Under the Tatelmans, and with Buffett's ownership, Jordan's Furniture continued to expand. In 2002, an IMAX 3D theater was installed at the Natick location, and a new showroom with an IMAX theater was built in Reading, Massachusetts, in 2004. People go for the movies and end up buying furniture.

Become Inspired

In 2006, after having officially worked at Jordan's Furniture for 34 years and unofficially for his entire life, Barry made the decision to retire from the company. His brother Eliot would continue to run the business along with the fourth Tatelman generation.

After retirement, Barry began to pursue his teenage dreams — theater and the arts — but continued to discuss promotional ideas for Jordan's Furniture frequently with Eliot.

When he entered the theater business, Barry was able to prove that his creativity never applied strictly to the furniture business. Indeed, that creativity is simply one ingredient of his overall success in life.

Barry's first production was a Broadway stage adaptation of the 1988 movie *Dirty Rotten Scoundrels*. The show became a hit and won a Tony Award for best performance by a leading actor. Barry hinted that he has been working on other Broadway-related projects, but he would not reveal the details until they reach the stage.

Barry believes that in any business, creativity and ideas can come from anywhere. A person needs only to remain receptive and friendly.

Creativity and ideas can come from anywhere. A person needs only to remain receptive and friendly.

As an example, he told the story of having dinner with a friend in the skin-care business who gave him some serum that would promote the growth of eyebrows and eyelashes. Barry tried it out for fun, and, after a while, his wife, Susan, and son Scot said that he looked different.

As the weeks passed, Barry's friends started asking him if he had had some "work" done on his face. He told them his story, and they wanted the serum, too.

Barry decided to team up with his friend and sell the product. RapidLash was launched in 2008, and it can now be found in major pharmacies.

A natural promoter, Barry noted that his marketing and creative capabilities have enabled him to take advantage of many new opportunities. However, he admits that throughout his career, his brother Eliot was the key person in monitoring the company budgets and finances.

In this regard, Barry admitted that basic accounting is perhaps a subject he should have spent more time studying. A good marketer not only is creative, but also knows how to produce promotions that deliver the biggest impact while using the least financial resources.

The Measure of Success

Barry is proud of the charity work he was able to undertake once Jordan's had become successful. A strong partner of the Massachusetts Adoption Resource Exchange, Barry helps to find homes for foster children and helps them receive a decent education.

He said, "It is a joy when you see how you can change your community into a better place!"

For Barry, success is measured not by how much money he has made but rather by what he has done with his life. He commented, "Of course I want to make money and to live well, but success to me is really about how to achieve a balanced life. For example, spending time with my family, doing well in business, contributing to charity, having good friends, staying creative, and also getting respect from the community."

"When my father, Edward, passed away in 1980, everybody in town came to his funeral to pay tribute. He died without an enemy. Money cannot buy that. Perhaps the number of people who attend one's funeral is a measurement of success," Barry added.

Barry and his wife, Susan, now spend half of their time in Boston and the other half in their winter getaway in Delray Beach, Florida. They have two children. Daughter Jodi was born in 1978 and now has two sons. Scot was born in 1980 and is busy setting up a nonprofit educational foundation.

Barry has always taught his children — and now his grandchildren — to think outside the box. "Always come up with a way to do things differently! You need to be creative and be different," he said.

"Consider what would happen if you opened a store and sold the same items as the store next door. Would you expect to perform better? If you do things the way they have been done before or the way they are supposed to be done, chances are, your results will be average, if not worse," Barry warned.

> *If you do things the way they have been done before or the way they are supposed to be done, chances are, your results will be average, if not worse.*

He further added that if people do not stand out and distinguish themselves by demonstrating creativity, then it is difficult to say on what basis they deserve to succeed.

Barry looked out at Boston Common and noticed some tulip bulbs. Although many may wonder what color the flowers will turn out to be, he said instead, "It doesn't matter. Just imagine!"

Chapter 5

Adding Value with Dennis Knautz

Acme Brick Company

"Mathematics is, in its way, the poetry of logical ideas."
—Albert Einstein

The Acme Brick Company offers brick and masonry-related construction products and materials to build houses and nonresidential structures in the United States. Its bricks are designed to withstand both subfreezing and extremely hot temperatures and, for home buyers, come with a transferrable 100-year warranty.

Founded just west of Fort Worth, Texas, in 1891 by George Bennett, Acme has sailed through numerous economic challenges since its inception. Bennett was an entrepreneur who, after noting the demand for brick in fast-growing Texas, decided to establish his own production factory.

During the financial panic of 1907, George Bennett died unexpectedly, leaving his son Walter, just 20 years old, to take over the business. In the face of a severe sales decline in a deteriorating economy and a number of labor strikes, Walter Bennett attempted to find a buyer for the company.

Then, however, a fortuitous accident occurred: an enormous fire in Midland, Texas, destroyed the entire city, thus creating increased demand for building materials. Acme began to thrive.

After selling a record 165 million bricks in 1928, the company suffered its first and only annual loss in 1934 during the Great Depression. As tough as the bricks it produced, Acme recovered and went from strength to strength. Following a number of careful acquisitions and expansions, its sales tripled between 1945 and 1950, rising from $3 million to $9 million in the five-year period.

In 1968, the Acme Brick Company changed its name to the First Worth Corporation. Then, following a merger with the Justin Companies of Fort Worth (the maker of Justin Boots) and Louisiana Concrete Products, Acme Brick took back its original name and officially became part of Justin Industries in 1972.

Under the leadership of John S. Justin Jr., who owned 20 percent of Justin Industries, and Acme CEO Edward L. Stout Jr., Acme Brick became America's top brickmaker in sales and production during 1976.

In 1999, Harrold Melton, a 24-year veteran of the company, became President and CEO of Acme Brick. That same year, together with Justin Jr., who was then in his early 80s and seriously ill, and Justin Industries' nonexecutive Chairman John Roach, Melton approached Berkshire Hathaway's Warren Buffett about the sale of the entire group.

On June 20, 2000, Buffett agreed to purchase Fort Worth–based Justin Industries for a cash offer of $22 a share, or roughly $600 million. At the time of the sale, Acme Brick accounted for two-thirds of the group's total annual revenue.

The year 2000 was seen as the beginning of the Internet age, and Buffett wrote in his 2001 letter to Berkshire shareholders: "I can't resist pointing out that Berkshire — whose top management has long been mired in the nineteenth century — is now one of the very few authentic 'clicks-and-bricks' businesses around. We went into 2000 with GEICO (an auto insurance company) doing significant business on the Internet, and then we added Acme. You can bet this move by Berkshire is making them sweat in Silicon Valley."

Acme Brick, now with headquarters in a 77,000-square-foot landmark building in Fort Worth, has more than 3,000 employees, 31 production plants, and 46 sales offices throughout the country.

Dennis Knautz became the company's 11th President and CEO in 2005, and has led the company's relentless efforts to satisfy customers by providing quality products and services, including the company's renowned 100-year warranty. The loyalty and commitment of the Acme team, which has stuck by the company through thick and thin, indicates that it will continue to provide value and sustainability to the U.S. housing market.

D ennis Knautz is the President and CEO of Acme Brick. A certified public accountant, he has been in the brick industry for more than 27 years. Although he has a good sense of accounting, Dennis looks beyond the numbers to improve Acme's operations one step at a time. He likes to advertise the brick industry by telling customers that their bricks will not burn *or fade even after a 30-year mortgage has been paid off. Dennis shared his story with humor and sincerity.*

Born in Chicago, Illinois, in 1953, sports and mathematics occupied most of Dennis's early childhood. His father, Donald Knautz, worked at a TV station in Chicago, and his mother, Norma, was a housewife who took care of him and his three younger siblings.

Although Dennis was heavily into football, baseball, and ice hockey, his mind was always full of numbers. He felt that solving mathematical equations provided excitement at school. Indeed, his math scores were always near the top of the class. Thus, it was clear to Dennis that after graduating from Deerfield High School in northern Chicago, he would major in the subject at college.

He had another dream: to play ice hockey at the collegiate level. He planned to enroll at the University of Denver because of its strong ice-hockey team. Then, during the fall of 1970, when he was still in his senior year of high school, a sit-in on the Denver campus to protest the Vietnam War became major national news. The situation worried many parents. Dennis's parents were no exception, and they asked him to reconsider his college choice.

Dennis recalled, "As I wanted to be independent and experience my college years away from home, Texas came to mind because of its perfect weather conditions and pretty girls!"

Faced with a choice between the University of Texas and Texas Christian University (TCU), he applied to TCU because of its smaller size and better teacher–student ratio. After arriving in Texas, he fell in love with the place and its business climate, and he has not lived elsewhere since, apart from a one-year stint in Idaho.

When he first entered TCU, mathematics was the obvious choice of major for Dennis. However, by the time he had begun his junior year, he was questioning his love for the subject.

He found the coursework to be overly theoretical and inapplicable to the real world. Instead, he took some elective courses to explore other aspects of numbers, namely accounting and statistics.

He remarked, "Accounting totally reinvigorated my love of numbers. I found the subject to be relevant and tangible. By learning how to analyze companies' financial statements, I felt that those numbers were in touch with the real world!"

Dennis cautioned, though, that understanding financial numbers is just the beginning. He would later realize that improving those numbers requires tremendous planning and strategic implementation.

Knowing that accounting was, for him, the missing link between academe and reality, Dennis considered majoring in accounting as well as mathematics. However, as he began to take on more business management courses, he realized that if he applied for the business administration program, he would need only one extra year of schooling to earn a master's degree.

He decided to apply and, much to his surprise, he scored in the top 97th percentile on the placement exam and received a full scholarship.

Becoming the Boss

During his university years, Dennis also worked as a part-time clerk at a local bus company in Fort Worth called

City Transit Service (CITRAN). He was a nighttime cashier at the bus station and an assistant in the accounting department.

Upon graduation, Dennis was uncertain about his future. He knew he was capable of accounting and business management, but he had no idea which business field suited him best. He also had not yet found any jobs with business management potential.

Then, one day, he sat down with the general manager at CITRAN and asked him for career advice. After their discussion, the manager unexpectedly offered Dennis a post as accounting supervisor. Without hesitation, he took the job.

In retrospect, Dennis believes that his transition from college to the real world was smooth. When he joined CITRAN as a full-time accounting supervisor in 1976, he already knew the operation, the employees, and more important, what he needed to do for the company.

At 23 years of age, Dennis knew that if he wanted to prove himself, he first needed to win the respect of his colleagues. He explained, "I worked as a part-time clerk at CITRAN, then all of a sudden I became everyone's supervisor. It was a mentally challenging experience for me. I had to dress up properly and act professionally. I was excited yet nervous because having the same group of people suddenly working under my supervision, I knew the expectation level would be higher and different. I had to prove my capability and win everyone's approval."

Although CITRAN was affiliated with the City of Fort Worth, its overall business operations were managed by a consulting group called McDonald Transit Associates (MCDT). MCDT managed transit operations nationwide, and all of the accounting executives from the various transit networks reported to the main office.

Dennis in His Early Career
SOURCE: Used with the permission of Dennis Knautz.

Responsible for accounting and financial reporting, Dennis had the added opportunity to coordinate with the managers at MCDT regularly regarding internal audits and management reviews.

After a year with CITRAN, a promotion opportunity arose in 1977: MCDT offered Dennis a position as assistant manager of Boise Urban Stages, the transit operation in Boise, Idaho. The new location operated a 26-bus system and would give Dennis more managerial and accounting experience. Still young and single, he left Texas for Idaho.

While he was on his way to take up his new post, which included a vacation stopover with his parents in Michigan, there was an internal conflict in the Boise office: Dennis's new immediate superior had an argument with the MCDT management team and decided to quit his job. The upshot was that when Dennis arrived, he was immediately named resident manager of the Boise operation.

In the following year, Dennis had responsibility not only for accounting and financial reporting but also for planning and budgeting, bus operations and vehicle maintenance, personnel and labor relations, and even liaising with city officials.

In 1978, the MCDT management contract with the city of Boise ended. Dennis was reassigned to the Fort Worth office and was quickly promoted to be MCDT's Vice President of Finance and Administration.

Now back in his favorite city, Dennis became more career focused. After the Boise experience, which gave him a taste of management, he realized that although financial reporting is an important duty, knowing how to manage the business is more crucial.

> *Do numbers tell you the whole story? Yes and no!*

He noted, "Do numbers tell you the whole story? Yes and no! They tell you how a business is being operated, but they don't tell you how it should be operated."

Growing within an Organization

Now dealing with senior managers, Dennis realized that most of the top accounting executives were CPAs. He knew that if he wanted to be promoted further, he would need the same professional certification. So, while working full-time at MCDT, he took additional accounting classes to prepare himself for the qualifying exams. At age 27, in 1980, Dennis became a CPA.

He said, "I knew I had the innate talent to prepare financial statements, but if I could do only that, I would be only an accountant. My next goal after becoming a CPA was to take on higher responsibilities. I needed to be able to extract information from financial statements, then set financial parameters for business review, and finally add value to the company by making proposals to senior management about how the business could improve."

Dennis readily achieved his objectives. With his new CPA credentials, he was instantly granted new tasks. For example, he was asked to implement a new management information system for the company so that its financial reporting, budgeting, and marketing procedures could be more easily conducted.

In 1981, Dennis was promoted again and became the company's Chief Financial Officer. His new responsibilities meant that he had oversight of all of MCDT's financial and accounting functions.

After a couple of years as CFO, Dennis then made a career decision to leave MCDT and explore new opportunities. He explained his rationale: "I felt that I had already reached the top point in my career as the CFO of this business. The total revenue of the company was decent and had further growth potential, but if I wanted to swim with bigger fishes, I needed to find a bigger pond."

Around that time, one of Dennis's former bosses at CITRAN, Bill Lemond, told Dennis that his new firm, Acme Brick Company, was many times larger than MCDT. As Acme and its parent company, Justin Industries, were going through reorganization to break up their centralized accounting and financial operating units, they needed a new controller to oversee the reorganization process. Being a CPA was a requirement.

Dennis was interested in the position because of its growth potential. Through Lemond, he was introduced to the President and CEO of Acme Brick, Ed Stout, who offered him the job. Thus, in 1982, Dennis became the Controller of the company.

Switching from a service industry to a manufacturing industry, Dennis had to start anew and learn about brick making. Although the brick industry may sound less than leading edge compared with high-tech industries, Dennis noted that the business put him in touch with many different disciplines.

He said, "I thought I would mainly focus on new accounting platforms, data processing, and credit and collections, but along the way, I also had to learn about the brick production process, which involves geology, physics, and chemistry; then I had to move on to inventory control, logistics, sales, and even branding."

Dennis explained that bricks are typically made from clay or shale. Once the proper mix of the materials has been determined, the bricks are formed and cut into shape before they are sent to a kiln. During the firing process, the bricks are heated to temperatures of between 1,850 and 2,200 degrees. During this firing process, they go through the chemical transformation before reaching a melting point. At the end of the process, chemical bonding occurs, and they are bricks forever more.

Referring to his job as Controller, which he held from 1982 to 1988, Dennis said that he worked closely with Acme's top managers to improve the company's structure from ground up via its accounting system.

By going through each step of the accounting process for brickmaking, he helped lead the company to a more efficient operation. When he started out, he could never have imagined that he would one day understand the company so well that he would become the most suitable executive to take over the top position at Acme Brick.

"My expectation all along was to become a part of the process, and then gradually become a part of the senior management team so I could plan for Acme's growth," Dennis said. "As a blueprint, my father showed me how loyalty to a single employer and long-term thinking could lead to a successful and rewarding career. He started out as a cameraman at Chicago's WGN TV station, then he gradually moved up to be the manager of broadcast operations. He shared with me his joy of growing within an organization."

> *My expectation all along was to become a part of the process, and then gradually become a part of the senior management team.*

Dennis followed in his father's footsteps by growing within Acme Brick. He joined the company in 1982 and has never left. In 1988, he was named Vice President and Chief Financial Officer.

When Warren Buffett's Berkshire Hathaway acquired Acme Brick in 2000, Dennis and the other senior managers were asked to help oversee the transition. In 2004, he was named Executive Vice President and Chief Operating Officer, and then President and CEO in 2005.

Being a part of Berkshire Hathaway gave Dennis greater financial flexibility to strengthen Acme's brand.

He said, "The extraordinary opportunity within the Berkshire family is the ability to keep managing a wonderful business, without worrying too much about producing short-term results at the expense of long-term value. With that, we worried less and could focus on the single goal of driving the business forward."

Dennis Posing with Warren Buffett
SOURCE: Used with the permission of Acme Brick.

Every month, Dennis has to send Acme Brick's financial results to Warren Buffett. Although Buffett occasionally comments on the figures and discusses the general business climate with him, Dennis said he tends not to bother the sage of Omaha much.

"Since Warren designates me to do what I do best, my rationale is to leave him alone as much as possible so that he can do what he does best — allocating capital. I talk to him seven or eight times a year," Dennis said.

Loving What You Do

Dennis emphasized that Acme has been around for more than 100 years. To be a part of such a legacy as a senior manager, he realized that his goal should be to improve and simplify the operation in preparation for the next generation of management. He runs the company with honesty and integrity and plans 60 or even 100 years ahead, because when a brick is shipped out, it has to provide guaranteed satisfaction to customers for a lifetime.

In fact, Acme introduced the industry's first 100-year warranty in the early 1990s, under which the company attests to the durability of its products and will provide a replacement to any dissatisfied homeowner.

He commented, "The brick business is not like selling a hamburger, for which the customer will come back again tomorrow. When you lay a brick, you probably don't need a replacement for years. We know our limitations, so we want our brand to be reliable and trusted."

To this point, Dennis wants his customers to know that Acme owns up to its mistakes, if there are any. He wants Acme to be treated as the industry's most-revered brand. With the 100-year warranty, his message is loud and clear.

With 24 brick plants, 7 concrete block plants, and 46 sales offices around the country, Dennis spends close to 60 to 75 days each year on the road. He has to be at the front line to get up-to-date information about the business. Because shipping bricks farther than 250 to 300 miles can be more expensive than producing them, the brick industry is extremely regional in nature. Dennis therefore treats every sales location as a small business operation.

By thinking locally and understanding demographics, Dennis is able to analyze sales figures and adopt various financial measures to adjust an operation's business tactics.

Dennis Celebrating Acme Brick's 118th Year
SOURCE: Used with the permission of Acme Brick.

In this respect, Dennis is well aware of the fact that he cannot accomplish everything alone. He said, "Teamwork is very important in the process. While I focus on the big picture, my senior managers focus on their areas of responsibility and the sales managers at different locations need to synchronize with us so we can move forward together."

Dennis admitted that the brick industry is no longer a high-growth sector and that attracting talent can be difficult. That said, the prospects remain bright for mid level managers who want to stay competitive in a traditional business, as long as they have a long-term perspective.

As a leader, Dennis has realized that there are virtually no businesses that can be fully explicated in a crash course. Newcomers to the industry must learn to be patient and take their career as it comes.

"Over time, an individual becomes interested in the business, and he or she becomes efficient along the way," Dennis said. "The true appreciation of the industry begins when the person has been tested through time and understands the heritage of the business."

He also views new employees as unpolished stones. Although their specific talents may be innate, it is the opportunity to ignite those talents that gives them passion for the job and allows them to excel within the organization.

Dennis never expected to find himself in the brick industry. He jokes that if he says he loves the brick business and is passionate about bricks, then he will obviously be speaking in clichés. However, the opportunity to apply his skills and talents — namely accounting and business planning — has given him passion for Acme Brick.

"Life is not just about doing what you love, but loving what you do," he added.

To motivate his employees and show them his appreciation, Dennis sends out hundreds of personally hand-signed thank-you cards each month and regularly communicates with his staff.

> *Life is not just about doing what you love, but loving what you do.*

With around 3,000 employees across the country, Dennis may not know everyone, but he wants them to know that there is someone sitting in the Fort Worth office who appreciates them and think constantly of their hard work.

Numbers Don't Lie

A loving father and husband, Dennis likes to spend time with his family in the open air during the weekends.

"There is a nice lake near our home. We like to spend a lot of our free time there boating and fishing. I'd like to play as much golf as possible, but that's only when my wife does not object," Dennis laughed as he explained. He met and married Connie Kempe while working at CITRAN, and they have now been married for more than 26 years.

Dennis has a stepson, Danny; and he and Connie have a daughter, Stephanie. Their daughter is an avid ice-hockey fan; she played soccer in her high school years and followed her father's path in attending TCU but majored in graphic design.

Dennis certainly has no advice to offer on graphic design, but he has been able to advise his daughter that basic accounting and business sense are required in any field. Dennis can talk numbers in as great a depth as anyone would like. However, he feels that if he had put more effort into legal studies, which often go hand in hand with accounting, his business sense may have been even more astute.

"Aside from legal studies," he added, "I was not too interested in politics when I was young, but as I get older, I have become more concerned about state affairs and government policies. It is a subject that fascinates me more at this age than I expected it would when I was younger. In many ways, I wish I devoted more time to reading, but whenever I have free time, my mind moves to financial statements, spreadsheets, and numerical analysis — whether it be financial, economic, or whatever."

Dennis believes that accounting has taught him some basic life principles. As an accountant, he has learned that numbers can be used to accurately tell a story, or they can be used to be somewhat misleading. Although numbers can lie to the world, however, they can never lie to themselves.

In addition, the essence of accounting is to report on a business operation fairly. The use of numbers and statistics goes far beyond accounting; they go to telling the story about the past and perhaps the future. Dennis said, "In the end, the numbers don't lie! So, truth, honesty, and integrity are virtues that every leader — and every individual — should embrace."

Chapter 6

Investigating Business with Brad Kinstler

See's Candies

"When you have eliminated the impossible, whatever remains, however improbable, must be the truth."

—Sir Arthur Conan Doyle

See's Candies is a confectionary maker mainly from the West Coast of the United States. Since its inception, the company has maintained a reputation of producing quality candy and chocolate. Its retail locations are all designed in classic black-and-white style, embracing the friendly and traditional way of candy making.

See's motto is, and has always been, "Quality without Compromise!"

The founder, Charles A. See, was originally a pharmacist in Canada. After a forest fire destroyed his two drugstores, See decided to migrate to California with his wife, two children, and 65-year old mother, Mary See.

To start his career afresh, See decided to open a candy store in Los Angeles in 1921. His mother, Mary, was a home confectionary expert, so he used many of her secret recipes. Mary See's portrait was even used in promoting the brand's family virtues and culture.

By the end of the late 1920s, See's Candies had more than 10 shops in Los Angeles. To distinguish its brands and promise freshness and quality, it launched a marketing program using distinctive black-and-white Harley-Davidson motorcycles for timely deliveries.

Despite the Great Depression during the 1930s, See's continued to expand. Charles See went to San Francisco in 1935 to explore its business climate, and he opened a store there in 1936. By the end of the same year, he had opened nine outlets in the city.

Most American businesses were affected by the Depression, but See's pressed on through the difficult economy. Its main challenges occurred during World War II, when sugar, butter, and other candy-making ingredients were rationed and became scarce.

True to its motto, See's refused to compromise with lower-quality ingredients. Instead, it limited its quantity and opened its shops for only a few hours each day. Customers who craved See's had to line up.

In 1949, Founder Charles See died. His eldest son, Laurence, took over and began expanding the company as wartime rationing abated and the American economy started to grow. He brought the company to a total headcount of 1,000 and expanded into 124 locations, with two manufacturing plants in California.

In 1969, at age 57, Laurence died, and his younger brother, Harry, assumed the role of President of See's. As Harry's main interest was not in the confectionary business, he decided to sell the company.

With annual sales of more than $28 million in 1971, See's attracted many buyers, with Berkshire Hathaway's Warren Buffett among them. In 1971, Buffett purchased See's Candies for $25 million via Berkshire's controlling company Blue Chip Stamps.

After the purchase, Chuck Huggins was named President and CEO of See's in 1972. He had joined See's in 1951 as a management trainee at the packaging department, and then worked his way up and rotated through various divisions, from candy making to purchasing and from marketing to management.

By the time he retired in 2005, Huggins had enhanced See's quality control and its product variety. At the same time, he maintained the old-fashioned charm of Mary and Charles See.

Brad Kinstler, who had been a Berkshire Hathaway executive since 1987, was handpicked by Warren Buffett to serve as See's new CEO in 2006.

Buffett noted in his 2007 Chairman's Letter to Shareholders: "We very seldom move managers from one industry to another at Berkshire. But we made an exception with Brad. . . . The move could not have worked out better. In his two years, profits at See's have increased more than 50 percent."

Now, with more than 200 retail locations in America, and franchises in Hong Kong, Japan, and Macau, 100 varieties of chocolate truffles, caramels, toffee, and other candies are served to satisfied customers.

Warren Buffett would always recommend a box of See's peanut brittle to start off the day!

*B*rad Kinstler is the President and CEO of See's Candies. Since joining Berkshire Hathaway in 1987, he has also worked at the conglomerate's other subsidiaries, including Cornhusker Casualty, Kansas Fire and Casualty, Continental Divide Insurance, Cypress Insurance, and Fechheimer Brothers. Interestingly, of all of the executives interviewed for this book, Brad is the only one to have actually applied for a job at Berkshire Hathaway.

In his See's Candies office in San Francisco, Brad discussed his experiences in business management and how his analytical ability has enabled him to try out different opportunities within the Berkshire Hathaway group.

Brad Kinstler was born in 1953 in Omaha, Nebraska. His father, William, was a piano technician, and his mother, Sharon, a housewife. When Brad was in kindergarten, the Kinstler household moved to Indiana to pursue a business opportunity, returning to their hometown during Brad's sophomore year in high school.

A top student who was strong in mathematics, Brad won a scholarship from a local engineering society to study civil engineering at the University of Nebraska.

He remarked, "I thought my strength in math would make me a good engineer, but after taking different subjects, I was not convinced a career in engineering was what I was looking for. I decided to take some time away from school, and enlisted in the United States Air Force in 1972."

At the age of 19, after taking a number of aptitude tests, Brad was assigned to study the Russian language: "Studying Russian at the Defense Language Institute in Monterey, California, was quite a new experience for me as a teenager."

Brad and the Author Posing with Grandmother See
SOURCE: Used with the permission of Ronald Chan.

For the next two years, Brad was stationed in Fairbanks, Alaska, where he was engaged in reconnaissance missions. He noted that his work remains classified to this day, but he commented, "The experience was valuable and gave me time to grow and become more focused on my future after the air force."

Upon leaving the air force in mid-1976, Brad had a clear direction in mind: he would return to college and major in political science. Although interested in politics, he felt that a degree in this field would lead to law school and a future career as a lawyer. However, life soon got in the way, which led to a change in his plan.

Brad explained: "I turned 24 in 1977 and got married. Soon, I had a child. At that point, I realized that law school wasn't going to happen because I had to start making a living to support my family. Ultimately, though, I got a very good baptism into the law when I later entered the insurance business."

The Making of an Analytical Mind

After graduating with a political science degree in 1979, Brad entered the workforce. High inflation and interest rates were hurting the economy, and the job market was poor. Brad had a difficult time finding a suitable job but decided to take an opportunity that presented itself. Through a friend's referral, he took a position overseeing the manufacturing process of a small company that designed and manufactured hog confinement facilities.

Brad admitted that this was "an odd job" for him, and, two years later, in 1981, he left to join the Chicago-based Alexander Proudfoot Company.

Over the following seven years, his work in the consulting profession provided him with a solid foundation in business management and equipped him with the analytical skills necessary to tackle different business situations.

Brad elaborated, "My job was to work with different companies to improve their productivity and efficiency. For example, I had to review the amount of time it took people to finish a job or the amount of labor [and] machinery required to complete a job. I then had to review and analyze the business process, and come up with recommendations to improve work flows and efficiency."

An important lesson learned during this time, Brad said, was that "from a management standpoint, the nature of businesses is much the same." As long as the business and its procedures are thoroughly investigated, ways to improve can always be identified: "Ultimately, a business is not only about sales but also about how to most efficiently run the operation and service the customer."

On the basis of his experiences, Brad believes a good executive always looks at a business objectively: "You can always find strengths and weaknesses in a company if you look at each component of the business from the top down and watch the details within the business. It is

It is about being logical and factual with your findings and thinking with the head and not the heart.

about being logical and factual with your findings and thinking with the head and not the heart!"

He explained, "There are times when a good product can be bad for a company. For example, if a product's sales do not match the energy and manpower required to produce it, then the risks and rewards do not balance out. From the logical standpoint, production may need to be discontinued. Although that's a tough decision to make, a good executive always remembers that in a successful business, you strive to do what is good for the owners, the customer, and the employees. When all are in sync, things generally go well."

Brad cautioned that, although it is important to make changes to improve a business, finding justifiable reasons to do so is even more crucial. He noted that companies often make changes on the basis of bad management reports and/or inappropriate performance measurements.

One of Brad's responsibilities at Proudfoot was helping companies design and review management reports. He learned that the first step toward improvement is seeking the right measurement tools. By coming up with the right performance criteria, companies can evaluate themselves objectively and make adjustments rationally.

Although grateful for the tremendous business experience he gained at Proudfoot, Brad decided to leave the company in 1987 because of the constant travel: "I was basically flying from state to state every week, returning to Omaha on a Friday night and leaving again on Sunday. After seven straight years of this routine, I wanted to stay in one place and eat my own cooking." Thus, at the age of 34, Brad applied for a job at Berkshire Hathaway, with headquarters in Omaha and one of the country's leading corporations.

In Search of the Berkshire Culture

"Working for Berkshire Hathaway was of real interest to me because the company is well respected, located in Omaha, and I had always wanted to be a part of it," Brad said. He sent his résumé to Warren Buffett, who passed it on to Michael Goldberg, a former McKinsey consultant who had joined Berkshire in 1981.

At the time, Goldberg was recruiting for Berkshire's insurance division. He was not specifically interested in employing someone with an insurance background. Instead, he wanted to seek new talent from another field to help review and improve its operations. Brad's broad analytical experience gained in the consulting field made him a good candidate.

After joining Berkshire Hathaway, Brad was assigned to work at its local insurance company in Omaha, the Cornhusker Casualty Company, focusing on the Property and Casualty side of the business.

"Mike said to me that 'you are either up, or out!'" Brad recalled. "He made it clear that I wasn't hired to hang around and learn about the business, but to excel and make a difference in the business."

Brad advanced quickly at Berkshire Hathaway. With Goldberg's constant encouragement, he was taught to think as a business owner and to act sensibly as an executive. Simply put, the company's business culture allowed him to recognize his true potential.

A Portrait of Brad
SOURCE: Used with the permission of Brad Kinstler.

Brad explained, "I used to report directly to Mike. Then, after transferring to See's in 2006, there was a slight change, and I have reported directly to Warren ever since."

Brad and Buffett do not have fixed schedules or regular business meetings. Every month, Brad sends in his monthly figures and reports what he thinks of the business: "If Warren wants to learn more, then we discuss it over the phone. Or if I need his advice or counsel, he's always available."

Brad appreciates Buffett's rational approach to handling businesses: "Warren looks at the long-term picture. Because he does not put us in the position of needing to achieve consistent revenue and earnings growth in all economic environments, we can shift our attention to the long term."

"Buffett does not expect a business to run perfectly from day one," Brad further added. "He understands that the road can be bumpy at times. When problems occur, he knows that the best policy is to fix them and move on, but he wants them fixed and not repeated. I expect the same as well."

Brad believes that by allowing Berkshire executives to run their businesses autonomously, Buffett gives them a strong sense of company ownership: "That gives us the confidence and passion to manage the business just as if it was ours. Our managers certainly feel that ownership."

Every company should build its own unique culture and business model. What works at Berkshire may not work elsewhere.

Having said that, Brad cautions against naively trying to emulate the Berkshire Hathaway culture. He explained, "I think an important point here is that every company should build its own unique culture and business model. What works at Berkshire may not work elsewhere."

Writing Million-Dollar Checks

At Cornhusker Casualty, Brad was responsible for heading the property and casualty claims and accounting functions. He said, "As my responsibilities grew, I had the opportunity to learn more about the law. I needed to understand tort law and insurance regulations, which differ from state to state, to make better judgments when it came to insurance claims and pricing risk."

While he focused on insurance claims and the accounting of the business, his colleague, Rod Eldred, now CEO of Berkshire Hathaway Homestate Companies, ran the front end, underwriting and marketing for the company.

By 1990, the two men effectively co-ran Cornhusker, as well as two other insurance operations — Kansas Fire and Casualty in Kansas and Continental Divide Insurance in Colorado. Although Brad joined Berkshire Hathaway to travel less, fate had other plans. As Brad's insurance responsibilities continued to expand, he again needed to travel regularly from state to state.

In 1991, Brad was asked to take charge of another Berkshire's insurance operation — the Cypress Insurance Company, a workers' compensation insurer. At the time, Cypress was based in Pasadena, California. Brad commuted there from Omaha for a year until a new office was set up in the San Francisco Bay Area.

"The new location became our central office, and when I was offered the opportunity to run Cypress, my family and I decided to move over. I was grateful for the opportunity," Brad said.

As company President, Brad was responsible for running the entire operation. He said he will never forget the massive workers' compensation claims he dealt with in those days or the hours he spent analyzing them: "One of the most critical aspects of the business was handling insurance claims. When you deal with multimillion-dollar claims, you have to expend an enormous amount of effort to understand the facts behind those claims and look to resolve those as effectively as possible."

Brad constantly had to determine the best solution for either defending or resolving claims at a reasonable cost, which required a thoughtful, balanced approach. "These are exercises that you can't learn from a textbook," he emphasized. "You ultimately gain experience through trial and error, analyzing facts and remedies, and predicting outcomes. Autographing a seven-figure check certainly teaches you the lesson that you are playing with real money!"

Reviewing his insurance career, Brad said the bumpiest years were the 1990s, when claim costs escalated, particularly in California, where local regulators wanted the industry to become more competitive.

He explained that the state's regulators removed the fixed-rate system and introduced an open-rate system to allow insurers to compete on premiums. "Although the scheme was beneficial to business owners," Brad said, "it hurt our industry because premiums were driven down by half, and the insurance model became unsustainable. We survived the storm, but many of our competitors went under."

The Turnaround Handyman

After more than 12 years in the insurance industry, Brad had proved himself to be an analytical executive. Not only did he maintain a steady business flow when Cypress was hard hit by the new insurance regulations, but his know-how in boosting efficiency and finding ways to reduce expenses also made him a versatile businessman. Both Warren Buffett and Michael Goldberg recognized these strengths and made him a proposition.

Brad recalled, "Warren had asked Mike to oversee Fechheimer Brothers, an Ohio-based uniform manufacturer whose clients include the military, fire departments and the post office. The company was originally operated by two brothers, Bob and George Heldman. After Bob passed away and George retired, there were some interim CEO's for a few years. Ultimately, Mike asked me if I wanted to take on the role of President of Fechheimer." Again, grateful for the opportunity, Brad said yes.

Headquartered in Cincinnati, Ohio, Fechheimer was a much larger company than Cypress Insurance. The Kinstler family packed up, leaving California in 1999, and headed back to the Midwest.

Brad went straight to business: "I admit that I am comfortable with going into a business that I don't understand a whole lot about. In my days as a business consultant, I was taught to analyze a company quickly and come up with rational approaches. As long as you know that it's a successful business and produces something salable, you can get things done."

To learn more about the business and the company, Brad spent a lot of time discussing operations with employees and learning more about their role in the company. Next, he turned to evaluating his competitors. He explained, "Knowing ourselves is not enough; we must also know our competitors! We have to understand their products and where they stand with respect to us. It starts with understanding your competitive advantage."

He noted that part of his mission at Fechheimer was simply to instill confidence within the organization about its prospects for the future and maintain stability at the top management level. After all, uniforms had always been a solid business, and Brad needed only to restore a focus on the basics.

At Cypress and then at Fechheimer, Brad continued to seek talent: "You can be a well-rounded manager yourself, and you can lead your company throughout your tenure. But if something happens to you, then your company can fall into crisis. Therefore, it is important that you build a good team of talented people. Finding strong managers with real talent is difficult, but essential to a well-run company."

Leaders come in different shapes and sizes, and it is often during a crisis or other extraordinary situation that their true ability emerges.

Brad believes that "spotting talent is more of an art than a science." He explained, "You'll never know whether you have an eye for it until you put your managers out in the playing field and observe the way they perform. What I realized is that there is no right or wrong when it comes to picking talent. In fact, you can't even tell who will be the next leader until he or she becomes one. Leaders come in different shapes and sizes, and it is often during a crisis or other extraordinary situation that their true ability emerges."

Warren Buffett indeed has an eye for talent. In his 2000 Chairman's Letter to Shareholders, he praised Brad by commenting, "We seldom move Berkshire managers from one enterprise to another, but maybe we should try it more: Brad is hitting home runs in his new job (Fechheimer Brothers), just as he always did at Cypress."

Quality without Compromise

In 2005, Buffett found a bigger challenge for Brad: running one of the world's best-known chocolate and candy makers, See's Candies, whose CEO, Chuck Huggins, was retiring after more than 55 years with the firm.

Brad recalled, "The whole idea really came from Warren. As the company was much larger than Fechheimer and the See's brand was so admired, I wasn't about to turn down the job."

After a year spent wrapping up things at Fechheimer, Brad became the CEO of See's in 2006. Once again, he had to relocate. He joked that he has now accepted his fate as a frequent traveler. At least the San Francisco Bay Area, where See's has its headquarters, was familiar from his Cypress Insurance days.

Upon joining See's, Brad inherited a company that was already in good shape: "The company has many capable managers who have been around for many years. They are an experienced and loyal group of people, and working with them has made my job much easier."

Because the company wanted to retain the quality of its products, Brad explained, it was not looking for cheaper or lower-quality ingredients to reduce costs. Thus, he had to analyze other aspects of the operation to find areas for improvement, for example, transport logistics, the candy- and chocolate-making production process, and the efficiency of the labor force.

Within two years, Brad had identified ways to energize See's by increasing sales and production, focusing on higher-margin products in some areas, and reducing costs in areas that could be tightened. The result: a profit increase of more than 50 percent.

Brad touring a See's factory with Warren Buffett
Source: Used with the permission of See's Candies.

Buffett said it all in his 2008 Chairman's Letter: "Kinstler says they simply make good chocolate less expensively. Part of that comes from vertical integration; by directly controlling production at its three California factories, See's can more acutely react to changes in demand. See's also doesn't spend a whole lot of money on product development or marketing. The product line doesn't vary much from year to year."

Although See's image may seem old-fashioned and out of step with current trends, Brad makes this defense: "Here at See's, we try not to follow trends. We have been making candy for almost 90 years. We know it's not essential to follow the latest trends because we have seen so many trends in our years of existence. We have realized that as long as we maintain our quality, customers will keep coming back."

The beauty of See's, Brad explained, lies in its heritage. See's continues to pass a taste for its products to the next generation. By maintaining quality and keeping that taste consistent, different generations share the same experience of eating See's candies and chocolate.

Despite improving the business through his analytical skills and a strong management team, Brad has depended on the brain but left some room for the heart. The most encouraging aspect of his job, he noted, is receiving fan letters: "A 100-year-old customer sent in a letter praising us for how we have maintained the quality of our products. She mentioned that the world has changed, but the taste of See's has remained the same. Each time she eats her favorite dark chocolate coconut cream, she thinks about the different stages of her life.

"It is amazing that one taste can recall so many different memories. That, to me, is really what 'Quality without Compromise' stands for!"

Chapter 7

Looking Forward with Marla Gottschalk

The Pampered Chef

"I am a slow walker, but I never walk backwards."
— Abraham Lincoln

The Pampered Chef is a leading direct seller of high-quality kitchen-related products and tools. It was founded in 1980 by Doris Christopher, a 35-year-old home economics teacher in suburban Chicago, Illinois.

With cooking and teaching skills, Doris and her husband, Jay, came up with the idea of The Pampered Chef "Kitchen Show," whereby Doris would soft sell kitchen tools while demonstrating cooking techniques to a small group of people.

Drawing $3,000 cash from Jay's life insurance policy (the business has had no further capital injections), the first Kitchen Show came to life on October 15, 1980. A church friend of Doris opened her house and invited nine women to the event.

Doris was nervous, but she demonstrated well, sold $178 worth of kitchen utensils, and was even approached by four other women who wanted her to conduct more Kitchen Shows.

In 1980, Doris hosted 18 Kitchen Shows and generated $6,689.78 in gross sales, an average of $372 per show. By 1981, the business had taken off, generating $67,000 in sales with 12 Kitchen Consultants recruited as the business expanded.

Still managing business operations and storing its inventory in the Christopher's household basement, The Pampered Chef moved to a 2,500-square-foot building in 1984, when revenues reached half a million dollars.

By 1986, sales topped the $1 million mark. Doris knew that professional expertise such as warehousing and distribution was needed, so she asked her husband, Jay, to join the group to overlook operations. Indeed, the husband-and-wife duo took business to the next level.

By the end of 1990, sales had grown to $10 million, with 700 Kitchen Consultants representing The Pampered Chef across the United States. A little more than a decade later, in 2001, the company had expanded into countries such as Canada, the United Kingdom, and Germany, with sales reaching $740 million and a total of 1,100 corporate employees and 67,000 Kitchen Consultants worldwide.

In 2002, not only did The Pampered Chef move to a new 780,000-square-foot international headquarters at One Pampered Chef Lane in Addison, Illinois, but a once-in-a-lifetime dream deal took place: the sale of the company to Berkshire Hathaway's Warren Buffett.

Doris and Jay had been concerned about a succession plan, wanting to keep the company's philosophy and heritage intact while selling to someone they could trust. Warren Buffett, of course, came to mind. The beauty of the business and the quality of its management led Buffett to buy The Pampered Chef for an undisclosed amount in October 2002.

In 2006, Marla Gottschalk, President and Chief Operating Officer of the company, took over the CEO role and has worked alongside Doris ever since.

Serving more than 12 million clients today, The Pampered Chef not only enjoys bringing families to the kitchen table but also aims at tackling three problems in society: hunger, family issues, and cancer. Through its Round-Up from the Heart Campaign, the company has helped fight hunger since 1991. The Pampered Chef Family Resiliency Program aims to understand and solve the many issues and challenges that families face today. The company also works closely with the American Cancer Society in its fight against breast cancer.

*M*arla Gottschalk is CEO of The Pampered Chef. At her office in Addison, an hour from Chicago, Illinois, Marla discussed her passion for her job and how she took every step in her career. One of only two female executives interviewed for this book, Marla showed her determination to excel as an executive and how the simple notion of staying consistent is an important ingredient of success.

"Your job is not your life, but your life consists of your job," Marla said as she started the conversation, "It is important to find a job that you enjoy doing. It may not be your first job, but you have to work towards finding your passion."

Marla learned from her father at an early age to search for passion in life. Born in 1960 in Bloomington, Indiana, Marla and her three older brothers grew up in entrepreneurial surrounds. Their father, Richard Curry, was a business-driven man who ran his own car dealership. Their mother, Patricia, was a housewife.

"My great-grandfather founded the car dealership. When my grandfather was in charge, he was more like a steward of the business. Then when my father took over, he was the innovator who brought the dealership forward by moving to a better location, expanding the service and body shop areas, and joining organizations where he could learn from other dealers who were successful. He was passionate about the business and was constantly trying to improve the dealership," Marla said.

Observing her father's dedication, Marla wanted to follow in his footsteps. When she was 17, she worked at the dealership part-time handling warranty claims. The process enabled her to learn the importance of communication, and she experienced various aspects of a business. The work environment simply fascinated her.

After graduating from high school, Marla was eager to enter the workforce rather than attend college. She felt that making ends meet was important, but she also wanted to find an ideal job through which to earn a living.

Marla became a bank teller for a while and then worked as the office manager at a medical clinic. At first it was fun, but after three years, she began to notice her weakness: "People who have high earning power tend to have an education. That was something I lacked because I blindly

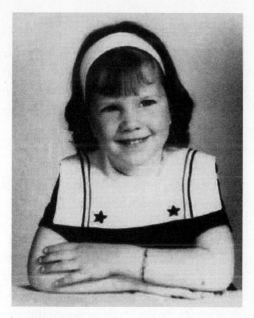

A Young Marla
SOURCE: Used with the permission of Marla Gottschalk.

entered the working world and hope to make money right away."

Noticing the importance of an education, Marla quickly changed her career plan. She applied for college and was accepted at Indiana University. She said, "Going back to school was a great experience. I was very focused and was able to use my limited work experience to help me in my studies."

"As a mother myself, would I recommend my children to do what I did? I probably would say no," Marla confessed. "The decision to return to school is often challenging because it takes some financial sacrifices. A person who wants to go back to school has to readjust her time, her financials, and her lifestyle."

Be Forward Looking

Higher education gave Marla a brighter future. She decided to major in accounting because the subject was essential to her career prospects. Having tasted the working world, Marla was considered more mature than her college peers. Although she had not found her ultimate passion in life, she nevertheless had a clearer direction for herself than many others.

"When I started college, I was already an independent person. I had my own apartment and had taken on more responsibilities. I knew that studying and working would be most ideal for me, so I ended up working at a restaurant and paid my way through college," Marla explained.

After graduation at 24, Marla was recruited by Peat, Marwick, and Mitchell, the accounting and consulting firm that became KPMG. As a staff accountant in the audit department, Marla was given lower-level tasks to review and audit various businesses. At first, it was an opportunity to learn, but she soon found her work to be quite mundane.

Marla elaborated, "It was a great opportunity to get a feel for different types of businesses at an entry-level position. I pushed myself to get a Certified Public Accountant license, but I eventually realized that my focus was all backward looking. It became clear to me that my interest was not about how a business performed historically, but how it should be operated going forward!"

A moment of self-realization came when Marla was assigned as a consultant to a real estate developer working on a shopping mall: "It wasn't the real estate sector that attracted me, but how I was given the chance to look into the prospect of a business. That was a defining moment for me when I knew that being an auditor was not what I wanted, so I decided to move on and find another opportunity."

Turning 29 in 1989, Marla made a career change by landing a senior financial analyst position at Kraft Foods.

She said, "The position enabled me to work with management in corporate planning. I knew Kraft Foods was a highly respected company and I was hopeful that I would have the opportunity to learn and advance."

Preparing for Opportunities

After joining Kraft, Marla was assigned to the corporate finance division. She was responsible for generating financial forecasts for various divisions and giving analysis to senior management.

Gradually, her ability was recognized. In the next few years, she rotated through a variety of division and functional areas. These experiences enabled her to understand the many facets of the food giant.

Marla said, "Kraft is a huge company with a lot of resources. Because the company is so big, we were encouraged to rotate through different departments and divisions to fully understand the company. I was fortunate to be given a lot of different experiences from running finance for the sales organization to overseeing investor relations and serving as Executive Vice President and General Manager of Kraft's Post Cereals division."

Reviewing her career at Kraft, Marla noted that there was no secret to why she excelled. She was simply being consistent with her hard work and determined with her career.

> *I was willing to take on less glamorous assignments if I thought I could learn from them and be recognized for my contributions.*

She explained, "I was constantly working hard and looking for the next opportunity. I was willing to take on less glamorous assignments if I thought I could learn from them and be recognized for my contributions. Taking on assignments in which things aren't working well is always an opportunity to shine if you get them running better. I wouldn't say there was a breakthrough career moment for me, but I was realistic with myself and I tried to move up one step at a time."

A Corporate Portrait of Marla
Source: Used with the permission of Marla Gottschalk.

To stay competitive, Marla decided to study for an MBA degree while working full time at Kraft. In 1991, she enrolled at Northwestern University in the Kellogg Graduate School of Management.

"The program blended into my career nicely because it allowed me to see the world academically and professionally," Marla said, "I was able to apply my working knowledge to the academic assignments. In addition, group assignments helped me to learn more about teamwork and communication. That made me a better leader as my career progressed."

On a personal level, higher education gave Marla more knowledge. On a professional level, she acknowledged that her MBA degree also gave her more credibility.

She commented, "Most senior managers at Kraft had an MBA. They advised me to get one. Their rationale for me was that if two people were to compete for a job opening, a person with an MBA would probably be more attractive than the one without it. It may not have been what I wanted to hear, but it was good advice and one of the best things I ever did."

While self-improvement is one aspect of consistency, another is staying firm to one's course and not being dissuaded by others. "Obviously I had a lot of temptation to switch to other fields and other companies, but I stayed true to my career because I enjoyed what I was doing," Marla added. "I simply found passion in the food business, and because I stuck to my career plan, I was recognized by Kraft and gradually moved up the 'food chain.' The outcome, of course, was landing my dream job at The Pampered Chef."

From Kraft Foods to The Pampered Chef

In 2003, Marla had an offer to become the President and Chief Operating Officer of The Pampered Chef, a direct-selling company.

She recalled, "I was intrigued by the company's product line because I always enjoy cooking, and I also admired the company being a part of Warren Buffett's Berkshire Hathaway. Its association with Buffett meant it must be a good business to begin with."

She added, "The truth was that I wasn't very familiar with the direct-selling business model [selling directly to consumers usually through home parties, group demonstrations, or personal contact arrangements], but I was quite certain that I could learn what made the model work and what made it successful. So in late 2003, I decided to take on the challenge and moved forward with The Pampered Chef."

Marla left Kraft Foods after having worked there for 14 years and officially joined The Pampered Chef.

With her solid business foundation, she quickly implemented strategic initiatives to strengthen and simplify the company. She also improved the product line and the business tools so that sales consultants could better prepare themselves when they conducted Kitchen Shows for potential customers.

With Marla at the helm, The Pampered Chef continued to thrive. In mid-2006, she was named Chief Executive Officer of the company and, although working closely with founder and Chair Doris Christopher, began reporting directly to Warren Buffett.

Marla noted how The Pampered Chef's business atmosphere was totally different from her previous job at Kraft. She explained, "The difference with Berkshire Hathaway and The Pampered Chef is that Warren Buffett takes a more hands-off approach. He makes sure that his managers know his expectations, but he does not play an active role in the process. However, Warren is always available for counsel

Marla with The Pampered Chef Founder Doris Christopher
SOURCE: Used with permission of The Pampered Chef.

and is willing to input his ideas whenever his managers need him."

Marla feels honored to be working under Buffett's guidance and receiving direct advice from him. She is also grateful that Berkshire Hathaway provides a stable corporate environment so she can focus entirely on business.

Working with founder Doris Christopher is also a joy: "Doris understands direct selling and she gave me a good sense of what's important to the business. She is an icon at the company and she is a role model for our consultants. She works hard, instills confidence, and motivates everyone because she shows that if she could succeed, our consultants can, too!"

Discovering Her Inner Chef

I get to roll up my sleeves and become involved in the business. Not only do I get to review the operation and make decisions, but I even get to become a better cook.

As CEO, Marla is involved in much of the company's decision-making process. With a relatively thin management layer, she is able to view the business clearly from all fronts: "I enjoy how I get to roll up my sleeves and become involved in the business. Not only do I get to review the operation and make decisions, but I even get to become a better cook," she said.

"I taste all of the recipes that we publish, and I also try to prepare many of them myself. It's almost like the acid test for the company because our recipes are supposed to be easy. If I have trouble making them, our consultants will have a difficult time, too. We want to make sure that anyone can achieve impressive results when they cook and entertain with Pampered Chef products and recipes," she further commented.

Speaking of her favorite recipe, Marla especially enjoys making the Tangy Pepper Pecan Brie (the recipe can be found at www.pamperedchef.com). It is her favorite appetizer because it only takes a couple of minutes to prepare and 10 minutes to bake: "Your family and your dinner guests think you worked for hours for that 'wow' appetizer," Marla added.

To Marla, the most important ingredient in success is passion; without it, life has no flavor. Although she has always held this as a life principle, she never truly understood its meaning until she joined The Pampered Chef.

She explained, "Eating, cooking, and working are three separate things. I never imagined finding a job in which I could tie them all together. Obviously, The Pampered Chef made that possible. Indirectly, I have become a better cook by becoming a better executive!"

The Need to Be Relevant

On entering her seventh year at The Pampered Chef, Marla thinks that the first rule of direct selling is to believe in what you sell. She said, "It is hard to sell if you don't believe in your products! With the variety of products we offer, our consultants get to choose their favorite tools to promote. Only by getting familiar with your products can you sell with confidence!"

Marla explained that her consultants pretty much set their own schedules, which means that self-motivation and discipline are crucial.

She explained, "As a direct-selling consultant, you are your own boss. You set your own goals and work to achieve those goals. There are consultants who count this as a side job, but there are those who are serious and want to make a living off it."

> *As a direct-selling consultant, you are your own boss. You set your own goals and work to achieve those goals.*

Reviewing the economy and the severe financial crisis in 2007 and 2008, Marla thinks that the Pampered Chef has become very relevant to consumers, especially during economic downturns.

She said, "When people look for ways to economize, they begin to realize the beauty of our company because we are selling great products and providing recipes that can save the consumer time and money. Many of our main meal recipes can be made for around $2 per serving in 30 minutes or less."

"Even more relevant is our business opportunity. With so many people losing their jobs, our opportunity provides a way to make additional income. So many people just need to make few hundred dollars a month extra to make ends meet and The Pampered Chef business opportunity provides that," she added.

Marla noted that people tend to join the direct-selling business during recessions when the unemployment rate rises. She feels that the business model directly helps the economy by providing jobs and opportunities.

Striking a Balance

Marla has a tight schedule at The Pampered Chef. Each morning, she looks at two key company figures: daily sales and consultant count.

She said, "Sales are important, but the amount of people joining or leaving the company is more crucial to me because consultants are our most important asset. Every consultant is like a retail store, they interface with the end customer and they are the ones who generate sales!"

"What I do each day is look for ways to help our consultants generate more sales and run their businesses better. I engage in a lot of meetings, discussing with top-level field executives our operation and ideas on how to improve our every facet of our business from our products to our cooking shows," she further commented.

Aside from work, Marla splits her time evenly with her family. In 1989, she married Andy Gottschalk, and the couple has two teenage daughters, Amanda and Laura.

Marla and Her Husband, Andy, with Their Daughters, Amanda and Laura
SOURCE: Used with the permission of Marla Gottschalk.

She said, "In life, I have two main focuses: my family, and my work. I am not that complicated and I solely focus on those two aspects in life. After work, I go support my daughters at their swimming practice. During vacations, we love to go skiing."

Marla stated that her secret recipe for life involves keeping things simple and staying consistent with herself. With her determined mind-set and busy schedule, she is living life to the fullest.

She exclaimed, "My advice is work hard, play hard, and never give up on finding your passion."

Chapter 8

Striving for Excellence with David Sokol

MidAmerican Energy Holdings Company

"We are what we repeatedly do. Excellence, then, is not an act, but a habit."

—Aristotle

MidAmerican Energy Holdings Company is a leader in the world's energy marketplace. Through its subsidiaries, the company generates, transmits, and distributes a variety of fuel sources to more than 7 million customers across the United States and the United Kingdom.

The company's history stretches back to 1971, when oil shortages led Charles Condy to form California Energy Company (CalEnergy) to develop geothermal power in North America.

The oil crisis became more severe in the mid-1970s, leading U.S. Congress to pass an energy policy act to promote renewable and alternative energy in 1978. CalEnergy subsequently thrived, winning numerous geothermal projects across the nation. In 1987, the company went public.

During the 1990s, CalEnergy decided to reposition itself and seek other energy sources to match growing consumption. Following the United Kingdom's deregulation of its utilities, the company acquired Northern Electric in 1996, subsequently providing retail gas and electricity to more than 1.5 million customers in northern England and Wales.

In 1998, it paid $2.4 billion to acquire MidAmerican Energy, which provides power to the American Midwest.

After the acquisition of MidAmerican, CalEnergy reorganized itself and changed its name to MidAmerican Energy Holdings Company in March 1999. In the same year, Walter Scott Jr., a major shareholder and director of the company, asked Warren Buffett whether Berkshire Hathaway would be interested in making a large investment in MidAmerican. After several meetings with Scott and CEO David Sokol, Buffett struck a deal with them.

In October 1999, Berkshire entered into an agreement to buy MidAmerican for $35.05 per share, valuing the company at roughly $2 billion.

In a statement, Buffett said, "We buy good companies with outstanding management and good growth potential at a fair price, and we're willing to wait longer than some investors for that potential to be realized. This investment is right in our sweet spot. If I only had two draft picks out of American business, Walter Scott and David Sokol are the ones I would choose for this industry."

Under David's leadership, MidAmerican became a powerhouse in the energy sector. With careful acquisitions and strategic energy diversifications, the company now provides energy to consumers via coal, natural gas, oil, nuclear reaction, wind, hydroelectricity, and biomass.

To date, the company's energy-related subsidiaries in the United States include PacifiCorp, MidAmerican Energy, CalEnergy, and several natural gas pipeline businesses that serve the Midwest and the West. In the United Kingdom, it owns CK Electric, which owns two electricity distribution businesses that serve more than 3.8 million end users.

Although energy is what MidAmerican represents, it also has found itself in a different field: property brokerage. Founded in 1998 in Minnesota, HomeServices of America was launched to provide real estate brokerage services to communities across the United States.

In just a few years, this division of MidAmerican became the second-largest real estate brokerage company in the country. As of 2009, HomeServices of America owned 21 market-leading brands and had more than 16,000 sales associates across 19 states.

MidAmerican and its business subsidiaries operate autonomously. However, they share a corporate philosophy: Put the customer first.

In their individual corporate mission statements, they declare: "We are committed to creating long-term energy solutions that benefit customers by improving reliability and cost efficiency while advancing energy independence and protecting our environment."

Indeed, the company has been true to its words. In 2008, the MidAmerican Energy Holding Company won several awards. First, J. D. Power and Associates ranked it number one for customer satisfaction in the Midwest. It then became one of only four energy companies worldwide to win a Platts Global Energy Award of

Excellence. To put this honor in perspective, a Platts award is to the energy field what an Oscar is to Hollywood. With more than 200 nominees from more than 30 countries, this honor for MidAmerican speaks for itself.

*D*avid Sokol, Chairman of the Board of MidAmerican Energy Holdings Company, is a man of his word. Although his appointment as interim CEO of Berkshire Hathaway's NetJets (a company that sells fractional ownership of aircraft) in August 2009 required him to travel around the country and attend numerous meetings, he was kind enough to fly from Ohio back to his hometown of Omaha in September to keep this interview commitment.

In a meeting in his office, he shared his stories and insights about personal growth, work, and the importance of self-discipline.

Born in 1956 in the American Midwest, David Sokol is the youngest in his family. While growing up with his five siblings in a lower-middle-income household, he was always taught to pursue his dreams. His parents were genuine believers in the American Dream and taught their children to work hard because America is the land of freedom and opportunity.

David's father, Ted, was a farmer who embraced the value of integrity. His mother, Marila, was a housewife whose top priority was her family. When David was 11 years old, his mother developed cancer, and his father changed careers, becoming a grocery store manager so he could spend more time taking care of his wife. Fortunately, Marila recovered and lived to an old age.

"My parents were always there for me," David said, "but they never guided me in a particular direction. They wanted me to pursue my own interests, and their expectation for me was simply that I get a good education and outperform them one day."

It could be the civil engineer in him, but when David was young, he always enjoyed building things. After his parents gave him an Erector set with wood, metal, and screws, he spent days building cranes, bridges, and skyscrapers: "Perhaps my parents indirectly gave me a mechanical aptitude for building things that led me to study engineering at college," he said.

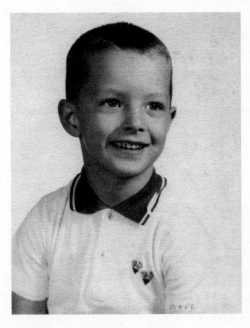

David in His Childhood
SOURCE: Used with permission of David Sokol.

Although David's parents constantly encouraged their children to chase their dreams, they were not the type to help them unless they showed effort.

David recalled how he once wanted to build a go-cart. His father guided him through the process but did not offer any other help. Although David was upset at first, he later realized that his father was teaching him the importance of taking initiative.

> *The importance of showing effort is a huge element of learning!*

David commented, "The importance of showing effort is a huge element of learning! If I showed my parents that I cared about what I was doing, then they would help. They wanted me to solve my own issues and learn how to plan for myself."

Now a father and grandfather, David has noticed that some parents today plan everything for their children. They focus too much on scheduling activities for them, which means their children may end up lacking the initiative and self-discipline required to succeed in the real world.

Seeing the Bigger Picture

David admitted that he was overly active in his youth, always attempting to juggle school, sports, and part-time work.

After his mother became sick, he looked for ways to help support the family. After school, he mowed lawns, baled hay, delivered newspapers, and even worked as a maintenance boy at an apartment complex. Those jobs taught him both people skills and communication skills and helped him to realize the importance of self-improvement.

Yet David said that he did not care much about his grades or performance in class. During his high school years, however, he received a wake-up call from his physics teacher: "Dr. Slocum was a tough grader, and he gave me a B at the end of the semester. I felt pretty good about it, until he said, 'Listen, David! You should be ashamed of that B. You are probably the smartest kid in the class, but all you got was a B.'" He told David that if he went through life being satisfied with Bs, then he would be underutilizing his talents.

"I don't know why that two-minute conversation struck me so hard," David recalled, "but it was the turning point in my education. It was the point when I became stricter

David in a Sporting Moment
Source: Used with permission of David Sokol.

127

with myself and no longer cared what others thought of me because I cared more about what I thought of myself."

After graduating from high school, David worked part-time to pay his way through college, studying civil engineering at the University of Nebraska. Initially working as a clerk at Baker's, an Omaha grocery store chain, he eventually was promoted to night-shift manager.

In addition to learning about basic marketing, ware-housing, and customer relations, David said that owner Abe Baker also taught him a very important business lesson.

Baker's slogan was "The Customer Is Always Right!" During David's time as manager, he said, a woman regularly returned expensive roasts, claiming they were no good and asking for a refund. Over time, it became clear to David that she was dishonest, and one day he refused to issue her a refund: "I knew I was doing the right thing, but right away Baker said we had to honor the company's slogan that the customer is always right."

David added, "He clearly knew this woman was dishonest but said what mattered was that other customers didn't know this and would consider the store to be breaching its commitment to its slogan."

That day, he learned that a company motto is more than just a saying: "I also came to realize how important it is to look at the big picture," he said. "I knew this lady was cheating us, but I was only looking at one side of the issue. I was doing something right on a case-by-case basis, but my actions potentially harmed the company's image."

Giving 110 Percent

David married his wife, Peggy, during his junior year in college, and the couple soon had two children, Kelly and David Jr.

To support his family, David found work as a structural engineer at Henningson, Durham, and Richardson (HDR), an architectural, engineering, and consulting company.

David confessed that he initially lacked professional confidence. He felt intellectually inferior to his peers and noticed that he was working twice as hard as they were to get his work done. He put this down to his feeling of always being the underdog.

"When I went to HDR, I was very disciplined and focused. When an opportunity arose, I gave it 110 percent because I wanted to excel. Besides, I wanted to make sure I was the last person to be fired because I had a wife and babies to support," he said.

Fairly soon, David came to the realization that he was actually progressing much more quickly than his peers. He understood his responsibilities well, and clients appreciated his work. However, he also began to find the technical aspect of his engineering duties to be repetitive. After all, the structure of any form of architecture — whether a hospital, a power plant, or even a prison — is very similar.

After a year at HDR, David sat down with Charles Durham, a partner in the firm, and told him of his aspirations and desire to apply his skill set more broadly within the engineering field. After that discussion, Durham recommended David for a position in the company's new independent engineering division.

"In the new division, I worked with commercial banks to help them analyze whether they should lend money to construction projects in different fields," David explained. "I was able to use my engineering expertise to advise them on the technological, environmental, and construction risks."

Still only in his mid-20s, the new position gave David a unique opportunity to look at projects worth billions of dollars. As a representative of commercial banks, he had to consider deals from a banker's viewpoint, requiring him to expand his business skills by studying finance, accounting, and law. Only by combining such business knowledge with his engineering expertise could he accurately analyze the viability of these huge construction projects.

Over the following two years, he worked with a number of different banks and analyzed projects in fields ranging from airlines, alternative energy, beverage bottling, and even power generation. "Looking at so many different projects served as a virtual MBA course for me," David said.

During that period, he moved to New York to work with Citibank on a number of projects and went through the bank's executive MBA program to learn more about accounting and finance. Providing services to different clients allowed him to look into the viability of different business models, he added, which "really helped me in the days ahead."

Gaining Respect

In 1983, David was presented with a new opportunity. An executive from one of Citibank's clients, the shipping firm Ogden Marine, called and asked whether he would be interested in starting up a new division on behalf of its parent company, Ogden Corporation. This new division would focus on waste-to-energy, or biomass energy, an area David had spent a tremendous amount of time researching for a prior assignment at HDR.

After additional discussions with Ogden, David decided to join the team, as the new venture would enable him to run a project from the ground up and become involved in an arena with immense business potential. Ogden Projects Inc. was officially formed.

Still just 27, David was suddenly faced with the challenge of leading a team of a dozen people at the new subsidiary, which was engaged in constructing new power plants. His first project was in Tulsa, Oklahoma, followed by another opportunity three months later in Salem, Oregon.

Over the subsequent six years, David steered the biomass division into a billion-dollar business and saw his small team expand to more than a thousand. Given its strong prospects, Ogden Corporation Chairman and CEO, Ralph Ablon, decided to take David's division public.

In 1989, David, then 32, became CEO of the company, which was listed on the New York Stock Exchange.

Although David's career prospects seemed very bright at this point, the fact that he unintentionally outshone those in Ogden's other units led to internal conflicts. Although he had Ablon's support to a large extent, the conflicts led David to resign just 12 months after the division went public.

He explained the difficulties this way: "When I was a 27-year-old project manager, I had to lead some older and more experienced managers. The reality was that some of them were uncomfortable working with me. The only thing I could do was to keep my head down, check my ego at the door, and work extremely hard to prove that I was capable of leading. I didn't try to convince them of anything other than the need to accomplish everything

> *The only thing I could do was to keep my head down, check my ego at the door, and work extremely hard to prove that I was capable of leading.*

as a team." It is clear, however, that they resented his success.

Looking back, David realizes that people like answers. When they cannot figure out why a person is successful, they tend to look for excuses rather than the truth. Unfortunately, people gossip and focus on the negative, crediting success to luck or having good connections or the right background rather than recognizing the simple truth that those who work hard and are extremely disciplined and/or talented are often rewarded.

"My father taught me that it is difficult to control others' perceptions," David said, "but I can always control my own actions, and these actions can, over time, alter those perceptions. I constantly show my colleagues that I am an active listener, and I make sure to explain my rationale for every decision and to consider their opinions. That is all I can do, because the reality is that it will soon become clear whether or not I am capable."

Any other way of attempting to gain respect, he added, comes across as artificial.

Virtue of the Midwest

David's disenchantment at Ogden proved to be a blessing in disguise. Shortly after his departure in October 1990, a former business affiliate invited David to join him in looking at some energy projects. This new opportunity subsequently led to the founding of MidAmerican Energy Holdings Company, as it is known today.

That business affiliate was Walter Scott Jr., Chairman and CEO of Peter Kiewit Sons', one of the world's premier construction companies.

David said, "I met Walter in January 1984 when I started the biomass business for Ogden. My first energy plant in Tulsa had a tight budget and in order to get the project financing from a bank, I needed to find a creditworthy contractor to build it for me. I didn't know Walter at the time, but I knew Kiewit had a solid reputation, so I basically called the company and asked to speak to the CEO. Luckily, I was put through."

Scott expressed interest in the project, so David flew to Omaha from New York the next day to meet with him.

At another meeting 10 days later, they struck a deal: "I told Walter the honest truth that I had limited capital for the project, and that I wasn't trying to be arrogant, but I needed a firm price and a firm completion date. Walter said he wasn't sure if he could get the project done with the amount I offered, but that he was willing to try."

"In the end, we came to the gentleman's agreement that if the plant came in under budget, he'd pay half the difference back to our company, but if it came in over budget, he'd take care of it." David said they also made a verbal agreement, sealed with a handshake, that if Ogden required more plants in future, Kiewit would be the first choice.

As it turned out, their first project together was completed ahead of schedule and under budget. When Scott handed him an envelope with a check, David knew instantly that he was dealing with an upstanding businessman. The two built 11 more plants together and became close business affiliates.

To David, Scott is a man of integrity and commitment: "I have told Walter a couple of times that he is like a second father to me. He represents all of the business virtues that I believe in: to value hard work and know you'll be recognized in time; to be a man of your word; and to do what's right, not only what's profitable. Walter has all of the old school business virtues that are difficult to find today."

Lawyers may be necessary these days, he added, but "when you deal with Walter, his word is stronger than any contract!"

What most strikes David looking back is Scott's willingness to sit down and listen to him, even though he was still in his 20s and Scott was already very successful. David also appreciates the advice the older man gave him when he was still relatively inexperienced, as well as the example Scott's philanthropy set. "He taught me to give back to society."

A Business Friendship

In February 1991, David spotted an opportunity in Cal-Energy, a distressed company that was engaged in geothermal energy. After discussing it with Scott, the two men decided to purchase a stake in the company via Peter Kiewit Sons' investment arm. David would subsequently become the CEO of CalEnergy and turn the company around.

Starting out with around $400 million in total assets, David gradually grew CalEnergy into a behemoth with more than $10 billion in total assets by 1998. The company also changed its name to MidAmerican Energy Holdings in 1999 to reflect its diversity of energy resources throughout the country.

David understands that his success at MidAmerican is not his achievement alone. Without a good management team to oversee different projects and make decisions collaboratively, it would have been impossible to grow the company so rapidly. David feels fortunate to have worked closely with his business partner and now close friend Greg Abel, who joined MidAmerican in 1992.

A Portrait of David
SOURCE: Used with the permission of David Sokol.

Abel, who has an accounting background, rose through the ranks to senior management quickly thanks to his obvious ability and sharp business acumen. After serving as CEO of MidAmerican's various business divisions, he became the company's President and CEO in 2008.

Speaking of Abel, David commented: "The business-friend relationship normally comes into conflict. I think the reason that Greg and I can work it out is because we separate our two roles clearly, and we do it openly and knowingly. For example, we enjoy skiing together, but when we get back to work, we make sure we don't slack off and expect less of each other because we are friends. Instead, we hold ourselves to much higher standards."

Because they understand and respect each other so well, David said, their relationship as both friends and business partners had actually become a strength: "We think as a team and often solicit disagreement, recognizing that it can be very beneficial in making better decisions."

Remember the Fundamentals

During the late 1990s, a stock market bubble was in the making. In addition to Internet stocks, energy stocks also soared to sky-high levels. Hindsight has revealed that many of these companies were cooking the books and telling elaborate stories to investors. David, in contrast, had the self-discipline to remain calm and not make foolish investment decisions.

Being out of step with the times, however, has consequences. "We were by any measure a large company at that point," David explained. "We were generating solid profits every quarter, and we looked at our business in a risk-weighted way. Our stock was rising, but our peers were doubling and tripling theirs. Analysts became critical of us because our stock was lagging behind."

Stock analysts recommended that David adopt a more short-term perspective, complaining that the company's projects were too long-term oriented: "One analyst said to me that we needed more 'deal velocity.' He explained that our peers, including Enron, were making two to three deals a month, but we were only making one or two a year. In the end, I was just fed up."

By 1999, David could no longer bear the shortsighted nature of the investment community. His mounting frustration, and a family tragedy (his son, David Jr., had just succumbed to cancer), prompted David to consider ceasing to play the analysts' game by taking the company private. He set up a special board meeting to discuss the possible privatization of MidAmerican and carefully laid out his reasons for doing so.

"We came up with a leveraged-buyout plan in which the management team would take over the company with debt," David explained, "but this would naturally force us to break the company apart and hurt our employees. We did not want that, so I phoned Walter for advice. Coincidentally, he was with Warren Buffett in California at the time and said he'd ask Warren if he was interested."

The following week, David, Scott, and Buffett met. After just an hour together, a deal was struck. On October 25, 1999, Buffett's Berkshire Hathaway announced the acquisition of MidAmerican Energy Holdings Company for $35.05 a share, valuing the company at roughly $2 billion.

"Selling MidAmerican to Berkshire Hathaway is the best decision I have ever made in my career," David exclaimed. "Dealing with the two most important men in Omaha – Walter Scott Jr. and Warren Buffett — I am constantly reminded of their business virtues."

Of Buffett, David said: "He has both breadth and depth of knowledge. He understands all sectors of business, and understands the logic behind each. Sometimes he sounds like he does not know much about the technical issues of a sector because he isn't actively engaged in it. But he actually knows a lot because he reads so much, and he has the ability to put all of his research and information together to come to rational decisions."

David (Left) with the MidAmerican Brains Trust: Walter Scott Jr., Greg Abel, and Warren Buffett
SOURCE: Used with the permission of MidAmerican Energy Holdings.

What I have learned from Warren is that one should never bring emotion to a decision. Business decisions should always be based on facts, data, and circumstances.

Having been associated with Buffett for over a decade now, David has become even more disciplined in his work: "What I have learned from Warren is that one should never bring emotion to a decision. Business decisions should always be based on facts, data, and circumstances. You can be an emotional person, but your business decisions must be based on fundamentals, because a business is only worth so much, and emotion can crowd out your business judgment. In Warren's words, 'you have to be disciplined enough not to swing at every pitch!'"

Pleased But Not Satisfied

David treasures new talent. Over the years, he has taught a management and leadership course to MidAmerican's senior executive team. Doing so has allowed him not only to strengthen the firm's corporate values but also to spot and groom young talent to become tomorrow's leaders.

In 2007, David compiled his course material into a book to ensure more executives have access to his management philosophy. The book's title, *Pleased, But Not Satisfied,* comes from a favorite saying of Peter Kiewit, owner of Peter Kiewit Sons'. Walter Scott took it as his life's motto, and now it is David's, too. This simple saying has a powerful message (and one that David's physics teacher long ago instilled in him): One should never be satisfied because there are always new ways to improve.

Although encouraged to dream from an early age, David cautioned that "dreams will never be achieved if you don't turn them into goals!"

> *Dreams will never be achieved if you don't turn them into goals.*

David sets clear goals for himself each year and regularly measures his performance against them. When he achieves his goals, obviously he is only pleased, not satisfied. And when things do not go as planned, he has the discipline to readjust and try again.

"Many managers grow stagnant in their careers because they don't set clear goals and continue to improve themselves," David explained. "If someone says he has 20 years of experience, this can simply mean having one year of experience 20 times. That is lateral experience, and it will never get you to the next level. The most important thing, therefore, is to set your goals so that you can have a new experience in your field every year."

Goals are achieved for any number of reasons — hard work, persistence, determination, or even luck — David believes: "Certainly luck has played a part in my career, but I believe that you can create luck over time if you stay focused — by working harder; by being more prepared, and by willing to do things others are not. Maybe luck is when 'preparation meets opportunity!'"

An avid football fan, David once dreamed of playing the sport professionally, but he soon discovered his limitations. That said, observing how football players get tackled time and again and immediately stand back up to have another go, he has learned how to become a more disciplined person.

"It is just the same in business!" David stressed. "You keep trying, and you can't be afraid to fail. You might have to fall down 10 times in order to get one touchdown, but that touchdown may win the game. The problem is, you'll never know it's the winning touchdown if you are not disciplined enough to keep standing back up."

Indeed, discipline is what drives David forward. He concluded, "Throughout my career, I have just kept trying because I know that if I fall down seven times, then I have to stand up eight!"

Chapter 9

Learning to Adapt from Walter Scott Jr.

MidAmerican Energy Holdings Company

"It is not the strongest of the species that survive, nor the most intelligent, but the one most adaptive to change."
—Charles Darwin

W alter Scott Jr. is Chairman of Level 3 Communications Inc., Director and Chairman Emeritus of Peter Kiewit Sons' Inc., and Director of Valmont Industries. A longtime friend of Warren Buffett, Walter became associated with Berkshire Hathaway in 1988, when he was appointed as an independent director of the company. In 1999, Walter's relationship with Berkshire deepened when it purchased MidAmerican Energy Holdings Company, of which Walter was the majority shareholder.

In his office, one floor above Buffett's in Omaha, Nebraska, Walter spoke about the American Dream and his passion for philanthropy.

Born during 1931 in Omaha, Nebraska, Walter Scott Jr.'s upbringing was as ordinary as that of many others who grew up in the Midwest. During the Great Depression, when unemployment rates soared to more than 20 percent, Walter's father — Walter Scott Sr. — kept his job as chief engineer at the construction company Peter Kiewit Sons'.

Walter said, "My family was considered more fortunate than others. Construction work was scarce at the time, so my father did not get paid regularly, but neither did Peter Kiewit himself. After the launch of the New Deal, there were more infrastructure projects, and life became steadier."

Walter spent his early years with what he called the Jones Street Gang, a half dozen kids who would play kick the can or capture the flag during their spare time. Stanford Lipsey, Publisher of the *Buffalo News*, was Walter's neighbor and also part of the group. Buffett lived across town, so he and Walter did not meet until some years later.

From a young age, Walter was fascinated with the building of public infrastructure. As a schoolboy in the 1930s and 1940s, he would often accompany his father to Kiewit's construction sites, and he spent hours considering how the construction was carried out.

These site visits also taught him the importance of education. Observing that most construction workers could only offer physical labor, he decided that going to college would be his top priority. His own experience of manual labor during summers working on farms and ranches, and serving as a survey crew rodman and chainman on Kiewit construction sites further convinced him of this course of action.

Walter in His Late Teens
SOURCE: Used with the permission of Walter Scott Jr.

A summer job on the Oregon ranch of one of his father's acquaintances gave Walter some ideas about what he wanted out of life. Enjoying his days on the ranch, he initially thought he would study range management.

"In my youth, my decision-making process was rather simple," he admitted. "I wanted to learn more about the ranging business because I thought it could open up a lot of opportunities."

When choosing a college, Walter followed in the footsteps of a family friend to attend Colorado Agriculture and Mechanical University (now Colorado State University). "My rationale was that if my friend had gone to that school, it must be pretty good," Walter said.

Whether it was fate or luck, Walter decided to abandon range management on the advice of the same family friend, who suggested engineering for its more challenging coursework. He also convinced Walter that engineering makes a person more logical, thus providing more life opportunities and the flexibility to make career changes.

Walter took his friend's advice, gave up his plan to study range management, and pursued a degree in civil engineering — a return to his earlier fascination with public infrastructure.

The Courage to Change

After graduating, Walter realized that his technical background enabled him to do many things but that he would prefer a job that would equip him with business skills while allowing him to apply his engineering knowledge.

His father's employer, the construction firm Peter Kiewit Sons', turned out to be the right company.

In 1953, at the age of 22, Walter moved back to Omaha and joined the company as an engineer.

"I learned fast enough not to get into too much trouble," Walter remarked. His first engineering assignment was on a manufacturing plant project for Continental Can, a company Kiewit would acquire three decades later.

The U.S. Air Force called him up in 1954, and Walter spent the next two years in Florida serving as an air installation officer, inspecting road and runway construction for the military.

Although the experience was neither eventful nor meaningful, this period of Walter's life gave him an opportunity to reflect and set clearer goals for himself: "The experience taught me that the courage to change is required if you want to succeed!"

He noted that many civilians in those years were greatly influenced by the Great Depression, had lost their passion for life, and were unable to adapt to the way the world had changed: "Their objective was to work for the government so they could get a monthly salary, and nothing more."

Walter joked that if he had stayed in the Air Force too long, he would have lost his motivation as well. However, he quickly regained his business touch after rejoining Kiewit, where he was soon assigned to the Monticello Dam project in Napa County, California — his first major project.

Walter was next transferred to New York to work as project engineer on a channel excavation project on the Saint Lawrence Seaway. It was one of Kiewit's five contracts on the massive program to expand waterways to allow large vessels to travel freely from the Atlantic Ocean to the Great Lakes.

A year later, he was assigned to Kiewit's Cleveland office to work on cost estimates for highway projects.

Reflecting on his early travels and the numerous learning opportunities the company gave him, Walter confessed: "I was too young to ask why. When opportunities came, I just went for them!"

At the time, Kiewit had grown substantially and had projects across the United States. Thus, when senior management needed extra hands on new projects, they had to move people around the country.

Walter Discussing an Infrastructure Project with His Colleagues
SOURCE: Used with the permission of Peter Kiewit Sons'.

Walter recalled that when he was asked to transfer from California to New York, moving his whole family from coast to coast on short notice, he was given just four days to settle in. Although initially a daunting experience, he enjoyed his work so much that learning how to adapt quickly became a strength.

By the time he reached 30, Walter had already been married for nearly 10 years and had three children. Although his wife was initially concerned about the constant moving, Walter promised her that each time they relocated, their life would get a little better.

And it did.

In 1959, Walter was promoted to district engineer, and in 1962, to district manager. Just two years later, at the age of 33, he was elected Vice President and transferred back to Kiewit headquarters in Omaha to work with the senior management team.

"Life to me is a journey, not a destination," Walter explained. "At every stage in life, I equipped myself with new skills, and most impor-

> *Life to me is a journey, not a destination.*

tantly, at every stop on my journey, I kept my promise to make a better life for my family."

The Kiewit Principles

On his journey, Walter not only gained tremendous work experience but also learned valuable life lessons from his mentor, Peter Kiewit.

Walter said: "Peter took an interest in me and guided me. He understood the contracting business and what it took to run it. Very often people cannot transform a great idea into a business because they lack various business skills, such as law, finance, or accounting. Peter was a successful entrepreneur because he had an innate ability for all of those business concepts."

Peter Kiewit was able to spot talent and had a willingness to teach. He liked to try out young supervisors on small projects to test their abilities. If they were successful, he assigned them additional duties, rewarding talented employees with stock in the company to retain them.

Kiewit also gave his employees autonomy and created a harmonious, yet competitive environment in which eager and smart employees could excel and rise to the managerial level over time.

"Peter spent a lot of time mentoring me, and taught me a lot of simple philosophies," Walter reminisced, noting that he will always remember Kiewit's simple but important comment, "We don't want to be the biggest, but we want to be the best!"

Kiewit's attention to quality has a legacy in Walter's perception of other executives. He believes integrity and hard work are of the greatest importance: "Integrity is about being completely honest and open in both good and bad times. Obviously, when things are good, integrity is easy; but when things go bad and one still has integrity, that's admirable."

> *If you have to constantly push someone to work hard, then even if the person is talented in many ways, it won't do any good.*

He also thinks that hard work is the basis for success: "Those who succeed are hardworking self-starters. If you have to constantly push someone to work hard, then even if the person is talented in many ways, it won't do any good." Walter sees the discipline to work hard as the crucial factor determining success or failure.

The Ability to Adapt

When he became Vice President of Kiewit in 1964, Walter was given responsibility for all construction operations east of the Mississippi River. When he was named Executive Vice President a year later, he was also put in charge of projects in the eastern provinces of Canada, securing many profitable contracts there throughout the 1970s.

The final year of the decade was significant. Bob Wilson, named President in 1969, stepped down from the post in September of 1979 because of a heart condition. Peter Kiewit died in November. Walter was just 48 years old when he became Chairman, President, and CEO.

Walter recalled, "Peter had asked me to run the company and take on a leading role a number of times. I told him I was competent and ready but explained that I may not run the company the same way he did because no one thinks the same. He respected my frankness and trusted I could take the company to the next level."

Amid these professional challenges, Walter also suffered a personal tragedy when his wife, Carolyn, was diagnosed with cancer shortly after he became Kiewit's CEO. She died five years later.

"I think those were my toughest moments," Walter admitted. "The fact that I worked my way through those events means I can probably cope with anything that life throws at me."

After taking the helm of Kiewit, Walter immediately landed several megaprojects, including a $426 million tunnel under Baltimore's harbor and $400 million worth of mechanical work at the Washington Public Power Supply System's nuclear plants.

The business climate for the construction industry changed in the early 1980s. Interest rates were sky high, and many companies were delaying capital investment. As a result, Walter found few opportunities to reinvest capital into Kiewit's core businesses.

Instead, he began to invest in a variety of businesses. In 1984, Kiewit acquired conglomerate Continental Group, which was at that time the largest public company to ever be taken private. In 1988, Kiewit went into communication services via the access carrier MFS Communications, and in 1991, the company acquired a controlling interest in the geothermal energy developer CalEnergy.

To manage these and other investments, Walter reorganized the company into two major divisions, one holding the company's historic construction and mining business, and the other holding the noncore investments.

"The issue was that we made more money than we could utilize within the contracting business," Walter explained. "As an executive, I was put into a position of finding good projects and at the same time, rationally utilizing the company's capital.

"After all, our company had been generating returns of more than 20 percent annually for many decades. As Kiewit was a private, employee-owned company, our shareholders wanted us to achieve the same investment returns. So, while our engineers continued to stay focused on the contracting business, doing what they do best, the management team tried to find ways to allocate capital on our employees' behalf so we could achieve similar returns."

Walter's strategy paid off. By the end of the 1980s, Kiewit's investment holdings accounted for almost two-thirds of its annual turnover. Most of Continental's noncore businesses had been sold in the late 1980s to finance the acquisition. When the packaging industry began to consolidate, Kiewit also sold it, exiting most of its Continental investment by 1991. In 1993, MFS Communications went public in 1993, and the company's remaining interest was spun off to Kiewit shareholders in 1995.

Reviewing his life-long career at Peter Kiewit Sons', Walter highlights his ability to adapt to change, which has served him well over the years, particularly in the contracting business.

He said, "If you think about the contracting business, every new project is technically a new venture and a separate business. First, you have to be open to the new project idea, then you have to budget its cost and estimate its potential, then you have to find the right team to work on the project and resolve any problems that arise, and finally you have to think of a solution for closing down or unwinding the project."

> *My job has taught me to always look at new opportunities, to be a flexible businessman, and to be willing to make adjustments when necessary.*

Walter further explained: "No two projects are ever the same. Even if you have to build a road in two different places, you are still looking at two separate projects. I think the nature of my job has taught me to always look at new opportunities, to be a flexible businessman, and to be willing to make adjustments when necessary. I have become very comfortable with that over time."

Connecting with Berkshire Hathaway

In addition to remaining open to business ideas, Walter always enjoys giving opportunities to new talent. In the early 1980s, he met a young man with whom he would later be very proud to be associated — David Sokol.

The two met in 1984, when Sokol, then CEO of Ogden Projects, awarded a contract to Kiewit's power group to build a waste-to-energy plant. It was the first of seven plants Kiewit would build for Ogden. Walter and Sokol became acquainted through the contracting relationship and developed a friendship.

"I think I am lucky enough to have met half a dozen people in my life who pretty much have endless capabilities," Walter said, "and David is certainly one of them."

When Sokol became dissatisfied with Ogden in 1990, Walter asked him whether he would be interested in pursuing some energy investment ideas on Kiewit's behalf.

Half a year later, Sokol pitched a geothermal energy company called CalEnergy. Kiewit became its largest shareholder and Sokol became its CEO in 1991. The company became today's MidAmerican Energy Holdings Company, a subsidiary of Berkshire Hathaway.

Although Kiewit later sold its CalEnergy holdings, Walter decided to keep his personal stake because he believed in Sokol's leadership and foresight. He became the largest shareholder and would eventually sell the company to Warren Buffett.

In 1999, Sokol decided to privatize MidAmerican Energy because he felt the company's business model was little appreciated by Wall Street. He believed privatization would allow him to place more emphasis on energy projects than on managing stock analysts' expectations. He discussed his plans with various fund managers and institutions, but also asked Walter whether Warren Buffett would be interested.

As longtime friends and office neighbors, Walter and Buffett got together from time to time over the years to share business insights. Since 1988, when Walter was elected an independent director of Berkshire Hathaway, the two had interacted even more frequently.

Walter recalled, "David called me on a Friday and told me about the idea. I told him I was with Warren in California at his sister's house. I said I would ask him about it and see what he thought. The following week, Warren got back to me and said, 'Let's do it!' The rest is history."

Berkshire Hathaway purchased a 76 percent equity interest in MidAmerican Energy; the rest of the company remains owned by Walter, Sokol, and their related parties. Because of the Public Utility Holding Company Act of 1935, however, Berkshire Hathaway is restricted to a voting interest of less than 10 percent.

In praise of Walter, Buffett wrote in his 1999 Chairman's Letter: "Walter characteristically backed up his convictions with real money: He and his family will buy more MidAmerican stock for cash when the transaction closes, bringing their total investment to about $280 million. Walter will be the controlling shareholder of the company, and I can't think of a better person to hold that post."

Walter, in turn, appreciated Buffett's business acumen: "He has an innate ability that is unique. He is a ferocious reader, and can recall a lot of information off the top of his head. The uniqueness lies in how he puts all of the information together and draws his own conclusions from it. This is not just in business, but in many other subjects."

> *Warren has established his own standard that is not necessarily others' standard.*

"It is important to see how Warren has established his own standard that is not necessarily others' standard. For example, his idea of a circle of competence stresses that one should focus on what one knows best. In today's world, many people think they can do anything, and then spend a lot of time finding out that they can't. Warren determined his competence early on in life, and he has always stayed focused on it."

Being a Good Citizen

Now in his late 70s, Walter has shifted his own focus mainly toward philanthropy. In 2009, he won the Norman Vincent Peale Award from the Horatio Alger Association of Distinguished Americans, an award dedicated to those who have made exceptional humanitarian contributions to society and who have shown courage, tenacity, and integrity in the face of great challenges.

The award was handed to him by his great student, David Sokol, who commented of Walter: "He not only represents the American Dream but also sets an example of involvement and philanthropy for our members and scholars."

Walter Enjoying a Moment out from His Philanthropy
SOURCE: Used with the permission of Peter Kiewit Sons'.

Ranked one of the world's richest people by *Forbes* magazine, Walter, along with his second wife, Suzanne, strongly believe that wealth should be plowed back into society to help to build a brighter future for the next generation.

Through the Suzanne and Walter Scott Foundation, the couple has provided significant gifts and personal leadership to numerous causes, with a special emphasis on higher education. At the University of Nebraska's Peter Kiewit Institute, their foundation has constructed a data center, a business incubator building, and a student-housing complex, and it has provided numerous scholarships to engineering and information science students.

Walter joked that he has no objection to helping senior citizens as he is an old man himself, but his attention to youths lies simply in the belief that if he can provide the younger generation with a good education and good moral values, then they will become good citizens in the years to come.

Walter has three daughters and a son, and Suzanne has two sons. Between them, they have 17 grandchildren ranging in age from 5 to more than 30 years old.

Having gone through so much in life, he has two pieces of advice for the younger generation: "Be healthy and be educated!"

He continued, "I have constantly told my children and grandchildren that the greatest asset they can have is good health. Without it, nothing can be achieved, so stay away from anything illegal and stay active! The next great asset is a good education: nobody can take that away from you, and it is the best private deal you can make."

> *When things change, change along with them. Adapt!*

Walter concluded by returning to the way he has adjusted to the world's ever-changing circumstances: "Life is tricky. Many things in life that you acquire can be taken away from you. Once you have acquired knowledge, you can dream, but keep your feet on the ground. When things change, change along with them. Adapt!"

Conclusion

Behind the Berkshire Hathaway Curtain

"The chains of habit are too weak to be felt until they are too strong to be broken."

—Samuel Johnson

After spending two years preparing and working on this book, my greatest joy as its author was directly learning from and interacting with various Berkshire Hathaway managers and directors.

Although every participant in this book is independent of the others, I found that they all share similar life and work principles. In this concluding chapter, I attempt to sum up those principles broadly.

I hope that you, the reader, will benefit from each chapter and experience the journey these Berkshire leaders have taken as though you were there.

Defining Passion

Warren Buffett often advises people to find and pursue their passion at an early age; otherwise, he jokes, it is "like saving sex for your old age!"

Before writing this book, I had always considered the pursuit of passion to be industry specific. When we think of what we enjoy doing, we often think of a particular field, such as finance, medicine, fashion, or engineering.

Since meeting with the Berkshire Hathaway leaders featured in this book, however, I have come to realize that passion can also be job specific. Satisfaction can come from applying and focusing on a particular skill set.

For example, Barry Tatelman of Jordan's Furniture noted that his passion is for bringing creativity to the business. He admitted that furniture sales was not an exciting business in itself, but the challenge of bringing fun to work and of thinking outside the box provided the most excitement when he was expanding Jordan's.

Brad Kinstler of See's Candies stated that his greatest joy derives from being analytical. Throughout his days in consulting, insurance, uniform manufacturing, and now candy making, he has realized that his passion has never been industry specific. Rather, it is about how he can apply his skills to turn each organization in which he is involved into a more efficient and productive one.

Stanford Lipsey of the *Buffalo News*, in contrast, enjoys his job because he loves his industry. The newspaper business itself is what attracts him. His satisfaction lies in bringing quality news to the public, generating ideas to sell more advertising, and finding new ways to attract readership.

Passion, for Berkshire leaders, is a driver for success. The German word for passion is *leidenschaft*, which means to suffer, then to create. This seems an appropriate term for Berkshire leaders, as they did not become successful easily. They are a group of extremely focused individuals who constantly work hard to improve themselves and their businesses.

It's Simply Hard Work

The term "hard work" can seem like a cliché, but it is indeed the defining factor that distinguishes a leader. Like a tennis master who plays the game so well that hitting the ball seems effortless, and whose countless hours spent on the hard work of training and practice go unseen, Berkshire leaders have created success because they have contributed an enormous number of hours to preparation.

When Cathy Baron-Tamraz joined Business Wire, she was eager to learn and to grow. She improved by asking questions, gained industry knowledge by taking up different initiatives, and has always remained receptive to new ideas.

Cathy excels because she cares. Her hard work may not be quantifiable, but her dedication touches the heart of everyone around her and motivates them to pursue excellence.

Likewise, it was no coincidence that David Sokol became a leader at MidAmerican Energy. He outworked his peers from start to finish, not because he cared about what others thought of him, but because he cared about what he thought of himself.

For David, there are always new directions for self-improvement, and he is never satisfied with his accomplishments. At best, he is only pleased with himself.

David admitted that luck does have a role to play, but success is also about being consistent with one's goals and remaining disciplined at all times. Luck, as he put it, occurs when preparation meets opportunity. His success can be accredited to what Thomas Edison called "one percent inspiration and ninety-nine percent perspiration!"

David's mentor, Walter Scott Jr., added that successful leaders are first and foremost hardworking self-starters: "If you have to constantly push someone to work hard, then even if the person is talented in many ways, it won't do any good."

Focusing on the Long Term

Berkshire leaders also understand that pure hard work means nothing if you do not focus on the right strategy. Building a sustainable and reputable business requires looking at the big picture and planning for the long term.

True leaders never look for quick profits or instant gratification. As Cathy said of Business Wire, "We are builders! We have the genes of going one step at a time. Maybe we are naive, but we really don't know any other way of running a business than to do the right thing and make sure that we can all sleep at night."

The discipline to remain focused also helps a leader to shrug off short-term distractions that may be detrimental to the overall health of a company. In this respect,

Dennis Knautz of Acme Brick understands his responsibilities well.

Dennis emphasized that as part of the Acme legacy, his role is to focus on improving and streamlining the company in preparation for the next generation of management. He realizes that, ultimately, he will be around for only a few decades, whereas a brick can last for centuries. He never pursues short-term gains at the expense of Acme's long-term value.

Randy Watson of Justin Brands shares the same principles. Randy focuses his attention on building up Justin's brand name. He warned that a reputation can take years to build but only days to be destroyed. Focusing on the bigger picture is therefore his main goal.

Randy acknowledged that the ultimate success of a company never depends solely on one person. Although he devotes his energy to long-term planning, he also requires his colleagues to work in unison and to contribute to the whole. Success as a leader thus also requires the ability to delegate and to create team spirit within the organization.

The Virtues of Success

For many of these Berkshire leaders, success is about doing what is right, both in life and in business.

A student once asked Warren Buffett what character traits are needed to succeed. Buffett answered, "Intelligence, energy, and integrity. If you don't have the last one, the first two will kill you!"

The leaders profiled here all embrace integrity. Walter Scott Jr. believes that "integrity is about being completely honest and open in both good and bad times." When business is good, Walter observed, integrity is easy, but the most admirable quality in a leader is the ability to be candid when business is difficult.

Barry Tatelman mentioned that he and his brother Eliot decided to sell Jordan's Furniture to Warren Buffett because of his honesty and sincerity.

Barry noted that Buffett's remarkable achievement lies not only in the amount of money he has generated but also in how he has kept his integrity and sense of fairness at all times.

The measure of success for Barry is not money but the achievement of a balanced life: spending time with the family, doing well in business, contributing to charity, having good friends, and gaining respect from the wider society.

Barry even joked that perhaps the ultimate measure of success is the number of people who attend one's funeral. A truly successful person is loved by his or her community.

Marla Gottschalk of the Pampered Chef believes that the recipe for success is being consistent with one's self and keeping things simple.

Marla, a working mother, thinks that a successful businesswoman must be passionate about her career and her family. Striking a fine balance between the two is what makes life fruitful.

In addition, she stressed the importance of finding an enjoyable job: "Your job is not your life, but your life consists of your job!"

Building Value

The notion of value is deeply embedded in the corporate culture of Berkshire Hathaway.

Although we may think that the company's leaders have always dreamed of becoming successful, that is not the case. When they set out in the real world, most of them had the goal of simply becoming a person of value.

By constantly improving themselves, they knew that opportunities for success would eventually come.

When Dennis Knautz joined Acme Brick, his expectation from the start was to become part of the process. He realized that success would not come overnight, and therefore that the best policy was to remain loyal to a single employer and work his way up. He knew that if he proved himself to be a valuable employee, he would be recognized in time.

Stanford Lipsey never thought about becoming successful early in his career, either. In fact, when he graduated from college, he did not even know what he wanted to do in life. It wasn't until he had reached his late 20s that he discovered that his passion lay in the newspaper business.

Stan said that the feeling of accomplishment he gained at the *Buffalo News* gave him the encouragement to move forward.

After becoming Publisher, he realized that bringing value to the company alone was not enough. Delivering accurate and relevant news is one facet of the value chain, but equally important is promoting good corporate citizenship by initiating charitable projects that improve the community as a whole.

As for Brad Kinstler of See's Candies, he believes that success will come as long as an executive considers the larger picture. Value is naturally created when he or she thinks on behalf of all of the stakeholders in the business: owners, customers, employees, and the broader community.

"When all are in sync, all will be well," Brad said.

Keep Swimming!

When I began writing this book, I did not know whom I would meet or what I would learn.

Since meeting and interviewing a number of different Berkshire Hathaway leaders, I have realized that the reason the book has become a reality is that I had the courage to begin. I set out clear goals, and I kept trying.

Now that the book is finished, I know that success really does come in different forms. There is no such thing as the Holy Grail of success, except a persistent attitude and a burning desire to achieve one's dreams.

When things look grim, what matters is the courage to keep going. When there is a slight taste of success, it is the discipline to remain on guard.

I recall walking into the office of Don Keough, one of Berkshire Hathaway's directors who gave me advice when I was writing this book.

Don told me that the secret of his success is that he has always kept swimming: "I started out in a creek, then I swam into a river, then into a gulf, and finally into the ocean. The environment kept changing, and all I did was swim!"

Don began his career at a small company called Paxton and Gallagher, which was acquired by Swanson Foods, then Duncan Foods, and finally Coca-Cola. Each acquisition was a setback for Don because he had to rebuild his reputation. However, he relentlessly swam forward. In the end, he became President of one of the world's most admired companies — Coca-Cola.

Another essential ingredient to success, Don added, is to become an interesting person. Before one can become interesting, however, one needs to be interested.

Conclusion

Now in his 80s and with an extremely successful career to look back on, Don is certainly in a position to offer useful advice, and thus he gets the last word of this book. "If I were a young person now," he concluded, "I would work my butt off and simply keep swimming!"

Acknowledgments

First and foremost, I would like to thank Warren Buffett and his assistant, Debbie Bosanek. Without their initial positive response, I would not have had the courage to begin the book.

I told most of the Berkshire Hathaway executives and directors interviewed for this book that I do not see myself as the author. Instead, I am simply the messenger and coordinator: They all told their stories so well and conveyed their experiences so vividly that my job was merely to compile the interview transcripts.

In that respect, I would like to thank Cathy Baron-Tamraz, Randy Watson, Stanford Lipsey, Dennis Knautz, Barry Tatelman, Brad Kinstler, Marla Gottschalk, David Sokol, and Walter Scott Jr.

Don Keough, a board director of Berkshire Hathaway, Chairman of Allen & Co., and the ex-President of

Coca-Cola, met with me personally and gave me advice on the book. The inspiration he provided led directly to the book's title. Knowing Don is an honor, and having listened to his Coca-Cola stories, I can now drink Coke with pride. "It's the Real Thing!"

In addition to those featured in the book, many others related to Berkshire have helped me smooth out the writing process. I want to thank the following people: Phyllis Dantuono, Gregg Castano, Michael Becker, Jeff Abelson, Malory Shank, Lisa Lankes, Gail Gawron, Hannah Farenkopf, Dotty Shaw, Sharyl Mitchell, Linda Breclaw, Barbara Tracy, Julie Haack, Mike Faust, Dan Krueger, Judith Larson, and Susan Aldrich.

Although determination and persistence were the crucial factors leading to the completion of this book, moral support was probably just as important in giving me the strength to persevere. My wife, Jacinth, has always shown unconditional support for whatever I dream of doing. She gave me the confidence to write this book. In more practical terms, she has probably reviewed this manuscript more often than I have myself.

I have always had unconditional love from my mother, Mylene. She constantly reminds me that as long as what I do is for a good cause, then it is worth doing. My sister, Jade, and brother-in-law, Johnson, have also shown tremendous care and patience, despite my occasional ill temper when experiencing writer's block.

My father, Chan Yat San, passed away before the book got started. He used to say to me: "If you never try, you never know!" So I tried, and now I know.

In addition to my family members, my work colleagues have also contributed enormously to this book. My personal assistant, Kit, helped out with the research on Berkshire Hathaway and its many subsidiaries. My colleague, William, helped with the photograph editing. He also indirectly came up with the book cover design. My other colleagues, Brian and Alex, made insightful comments on the book's overall content and theme. My work affiliate, Julie Sung, helped with initial planning of this writing project.

My personal editors, Mike Poole and Erika Hebblethwaite, have perfected my use of the English language. They have given me well-balanced advice, as Mike always speaks from the masculine angle, and Erika evaluates everything from the feminine perspective. Working closely with them has enabled me to become a better writer and has helped me develop my own writing style.

I would also like to give special thanks to Terence Hsu and Gordon Chan for coordinating and organizing my trips to the United States. They also provided lodging and transportation while I was in California. Without them, my meetings would not have gone as efficiently.

Last, but not least, I would like to thank those who have worked closely with me at John Wiley & Sons. My editorial director, Debra Englander, has tremendous experience in the publishing industry. Because Debra was already familiar with Berkshire Hathaway and Warren Buffett, I was able to get straight to the point with her, which saved me a lot of time and effort in explaining the book's concept and theme. Debra also has an energetic team of editors and assistants, including Kelly O'Connor (developmental editor), Sharon Polese (marketing manager), Adriana Johnson (editorial assistant), Todd Tedesco (senior production editor), and Larry Fox (project manager).

All in all, this book has not really been an individual endeavor but rather a team effort. I would not have been able to turn this dream into a reality without the contribution of everyone mentioned here. Thank you all!

About the Author

Ronald W. Chan is the founder and CEO of Chartwell Capital Limited, an investment management company based in Hong Kong. He is a frequent contributor to financial newspapers and magazines in the Asia Pacific region. Ronald received his Bachelor of Science degrees in finance and accounting from New York University in 2002.

Index

Index

Index